THE CAMEL IN THE FOREST

A Memoir from the Israeli-Palestinian Conflict

A. E. HAYOUN

NEGEV PUBLISHING

All rights reserved. No part of this publication may be reproduced, stored, or transmitted in any form or by any means, electronic, mechanical, photocopying, recording, scanning, or otherwise without written permission from the publisher or the author, except as permitted by U.S. copyright law. It is illegal to copy this book, post it to a website, or distribute it by any other means without permission.

A. E. Hayoun asserts the moral right to be identified as the author of this work. The events and conversations in this book have been set down to the best of the author's ability, although some names and details have been changed to protect the privacy of individuals.

Copyright © 2021 by A. E. Hayoun

First paperback edition July 2024

Book Cover Painting by Kelly Colbert
Book Cover Design and Map by A. E. Hayoun

ISBN 979-898-904-1404 (paperback)

ISBN 979-898-904-1428 (eBook)

www.aehayoun.com
www.negcvpublishing.com

To my love,
For the shared, the given, and all that is to come.

TABLE OF CONTENTS

AUTHOR'S NOTE	1
EPIGRAPH	5
MAP	7
PROLOGUE	9

PART ONE: HOME

ARRIVING	13
BEGINNING	15
BAYIT	16
SPARROWS	18
AGAIN	19
WRITER ON THE ROOF	20
GARDEN	21
KITCHEN	23
NEIGHBORS	25
LEMON	26
COMPOST	27
PARDES	28
ISRAELIT	30
NEGEVIM	31
CAMEL	33
MISSING	34
SHUK	35
HUTZPA	39
WINE	41
PETIT PAYS	42
EXCAVATION	43
MALKA	45
SHABBAT	47
TAVOR	49
BINOCULARS	50
DANCE	51
CONTRARY	52
JOURNEY	53
NIGHT	54

PART TWO: DESERT

FOREST	59
KAN	60
UNDERGROUND	61
CHOSEN	62
RISHONOT	63
EVANIM	65
FURNACE	66
POTTERY	67
LAMBS	69
GIVAT OGER	71
POCKET LUGGAGE	73
SULIEMAN	74
CAVES	77
HADRA	78
KALANIYOT	81
REFUSE	82
NAMELESS	83
BOYS	84
INSECTS	86
SHEPHERDING	88
SPECIAL	90
WRITTEN	92
CHASE	93
TREASURE	96
WADI	97
HIRAN	99
BIRTH	100
DUST	102
IRIS	103
RUIN	104
DUNE	106
EUCALYPTUS	107
GMALIM	108
REPORT	111
DESERTESS	113
HORVAT YATIR	114
GIVING	115
PILLAR	117
TZAVOA	118
HORVAT ANIM	120
SAKIN	122

Mushrooms	124
Ages	125
Eyes	126
Bereshit Sheli	127
Rumblings	129

PART THREE: WAR

PICTURES	135
SECURE	137
MATTER	138
DIG	139
CURFEW	140
SENSITIVE	142
HATIKVA	144
ENOUGH	147
ENEMY	148
LEARN	149
INHERITANCE	151
AVUD	153
WITNESS	155
WAILING	158
INDIGENOUS	160
SHAVUOT	163
AGREED	164
VAROD	165
PAWN	166
SHAWATI	167
CONQUEROR	169
LEVAVOT	171
APARTHEID	174
UGANDA	175
FREEDOM	177
BEDOUIN	178
AL-NAKBA	180
GVULOT	181
VOTE	182
CEASEFIRE	184
SHOFET SHOCHET	185
END	187
MEMORIAL	188
BALFOUR	189
AL-AQSA	190

evil is clearly demarcated and those who stand for goodness and truth are willing to work to preserve them against the constant onslaught of evil.

This story, my story, is just one perspective of life in Israel. Far too many stories of lives lived in this country will never be told and I honor their stories and their memories in the telling of my own. I have done my best to preserve the chronological accuracy of this book despite proofreading the final draft under the current circumstances so different and more difficult from the ones I originally wrote this book. Now three years, several wars, and many kilometers of walking later, *The Camel in the Forest* is finished and I hope it will highlight the importance of Israel not only as the Indigenous land of the Jewish people but also its significance as the only democracy in the Middle East. Israel's existence is not only of the utmost importance to the Jewish people but to the rest of the world and is a key component for any future of true peace in the Middle East. *The Camel in the Forest* is my statement of allegiance to this country I love, my devotion to it, and my fervent belief in its endurance and prosperity.

A. E. HAYOUN

אדר ב' תשפ"ד March 2024

הרוצה להחכים ידרים להעשיר יצפין - בבא בתרא כ"ה ב

One who wishes to become wise should face south and one who wishes to become wealthy should face north. – *Bava Batra 25b*

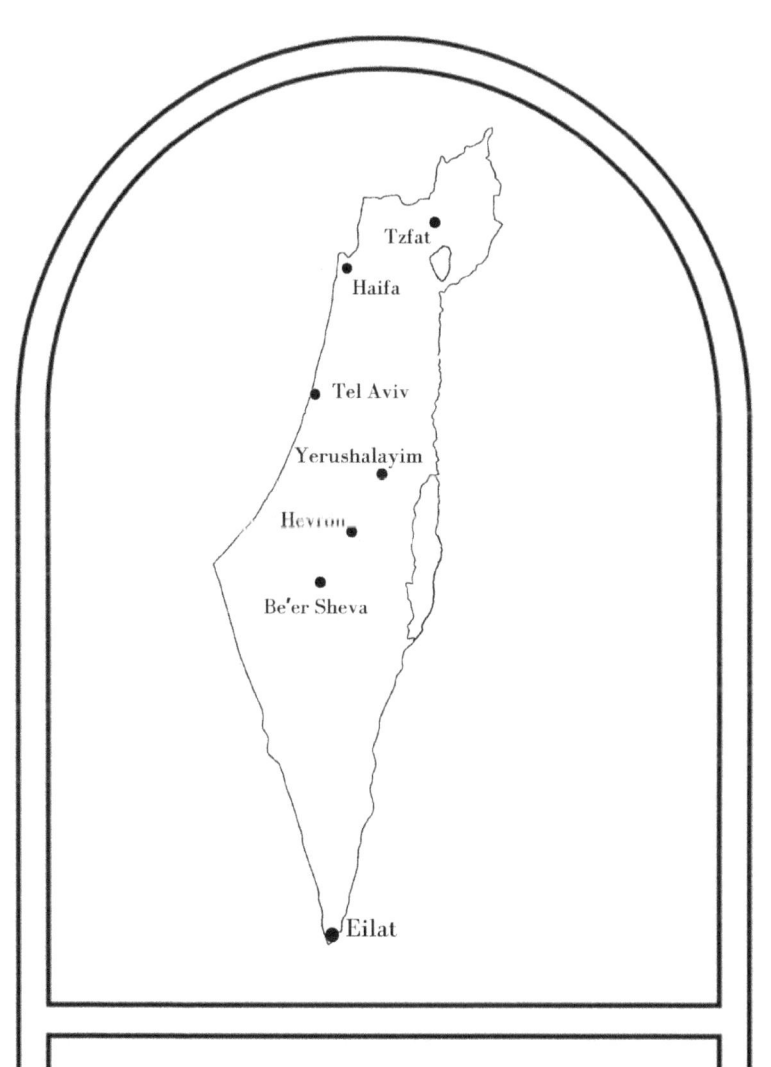

- Tzfat
- Haifa
- Tel Aviv
- Yerushalayim
- Hevron
- Be'er Sheva
- Eilat

Israel

PROLOGUE

In the moment of farewell, there was silence.
There was no feeling of leaving
Only a feeling of self being crushed and remolded,
Shaped into something both familiar and wholly new.

My feet dug deeper into the land they knew,
Trying to keep me rooted in the familiar.
But as the fear and doubt rushed out of me,
My feet took flight and I became weightless in the air.
My eyes looked forward into a tunnel of time and space,
Through the clouds and into the heavens.
Flying, rising, and falling between air pockets of doubt and hope.
There between heaven and earth,
I was homeless, borderless, and brave.

Then I saw it through a break in the clouds,
A glimpse of home, changed like a lover after years of absence,
Not as I remembered it but like a lover in the ways that matter,
In the essence, the shimmer, and the relentless desire.
The coastline, the sun, Jerusalem stone, and the sea.
Home was before me, a new life was beginning,
Shimmering through my tears was my lover in white and gold.

Home

I count my wealth in fruit and flowers

A. E. Hayoun

Arriving

Leaving home like a baby from the womb,
Screaming and leaving, arriving, and weeping,
Arriving home to the place I belong.
My hands carry luggage that contains my whole life,
And wrapped around my chest is my baby
Just arrived from my womb.

I am questioned, labeled, patted, and prodded,
As I pass through tunnel after tunnel.
I distantly hear, "Welcome to Izrael."
Finally emerging into the great chamber of arrivals,
I fumble forward, struggling
Under the weight of my child, my luggage, and my heart,
For the sake of all that I carry,
I push forward under the weight,
All the while my eyes search for home.

When suddenly the strong arms of home are encircling me,
Grasping me tight to his chest, the chest I know so well.
Between us, crushed in our embrace, our baby cries.
The hands of family take my luggage from me,
While his gently unwrap our baby from my body.
Imprinted on my chest is the shape of his little baby ear
And my necklace embossed on his little face.

In my mouth is honey and goat cheese, bread, and coffee,
In my ears are words half-heard,
"Welcome home, welcome home"
No longer on my own, my luggage is now ours
And there is family to cherish my baby.
As months of baggage are stripped
From my mind and body, I begin to float upwards.

In the midst of joyous celebration,
No one notices as my feet leave the stones.
My baby rests in comforting arms,
My husband leads us towards our new home,
But beyond the chatter and laughter and plans,

The Camel in the Forest

I am flying above the sea, sand, and stones.

Flying towards the sun, I am happy and free.
To the East, Jerusalem, to my left the fertile North,
And like a magnet, I am drawn South
Towards sand and baked earth.
The wind catches me and oh, how I fly!
Past Hevron and over Shfalim,
Towards the Gateway of the Negev.
Floating on my back, I gaze at the sun.

As I come back down to earth,
To my new home in this ancient land,
I see the sun I knew changed
To one that is brighter and whiter.
It moves over me like a beacon
To set behind me in the West.
And with the sunset, I send my love
Back to my mother and her womb I once called home.

A. E. Hayoun

BEGINNING

When did it begin, this great love of mine?
A love nestled deep in my chest,
Next to my knowledge of self,
The unforgettable moment I met my husband,
And the wonderous day my child was born.
My love of Israel has spanned my lifetime.

Did it begin with the Bible stories,
Of a little, great people following HaShem in the desert?
Or was it the first time I saw Hebrew letters,
Their curls and scrolls folding into me?
Maybe it was the pictures of oranges in Yafo, the salt sea,
Camels under date trees, or Jerusalem of gold?
It must have been the first time visiting as a girl,
And seeing the Mediterranean, the sun, and the desert,
Eating the Israeli chocolate and hummus.
It all traveled back home with me,
Assuring me I would return,
To return to my people,
To look deeper into the desert,
And to speak the language of Dinah and David.

I carried it with me everywhere, this love.
In university, I related every essay back to Israel,
Every presentation was on its right to exist.
I was defending my homeland
Before I could even truly call it home.
Aligning everything in my life to that one great desire,
To be a part of am hofshi b'artzenu
And if necessary, to leave everything else behind.
Far from leaving everything behind,
I brought with me the most important things.
Now in my arms, I cradle my son,
We sit together in the courtyard of our new home,
Under this beloved ancient sun.
My tea grows cold as I watch new birds.
My heart warms to the sounds of the Negev Deserts in Israel.

BAYIT

The house has been built, but the home takes time.
Place and shelter, full of objects and comfort.
My spirit has arrived home
But my body feels awkward here,
Finding its way around a new house.
No smell familiar, there is new food in the fridge,
And nothing that reminds me of life before.
In an unfamiliar bed, resting my head on a new pillow
There is an awkwardness between us
As I crush myself into it,
Trying to find a familiar indentation,
But the pillow pushes me away like a chastising lover.

Influenced by a different clock,
My body wakes hours before sunrise,
The birds are still sleeping in their Middle Eastern nests.
I begin with a coffee, fumbling for the kettle,
And searching for the teaspoons.
Rifling through cupboards and drawers,
I feel like an invader in my own home.
As I find everything I need the water begins to boil.
I pull the milk from the fridge and flush with excitement,
Excitement at the proverbial milk that flows in The Land.
I pour it into my coffee and it swirls creamily.
In the gradual dawn, I take the first sip
Of strong Israeli coffee and Holy Land milk,
And then I turn towards my luggage.

My luggage is comprised of the large lumpy shapes
On the floor in the receding darkness of home.
I know each one intimately
And which pieces of my previous life they hold.
Remnants, comforts, and objects of importance only to me.
Packed by the hands of my mother and sister,
Soaked in her tears and wrapped in their love.

The one I open first is the one I know best.
Its weary seams are ready to complete their mission

Of carrying the remains of my library halfway around the world.
The most beloved books from twenty-five years of reading
Plucked and peeled, chopped, and boiled down
To the core of personal literacy.

The birds are singing loudly now,
The sun begins to warm the concrete walls,
And I have finished my coffee.
My books stand together on a shelf in the living room,
The first objects with which to build a home,
My baby cries and a new day begins.

SPARROWS

The morning birds sing, but not the ones I know.
I hear the chirps, shrieks, and caws of birds I have not met.
But the sparrows, home everywhere in the world,
Chirp their morning song in the courtyard,
A familiar song but one I now hear differently
In the new air and stronger sunlight.

They eat crumbs from the table
And drink from stone floor puddles.
They swoop low and gather
In the trees of lemon, loquat, and tangerine.
They are comfortable in this garden
That was theirs before it became mine.

For an hour between six and seven,
The sparrows chatter in the evening branches
Until they drift off to sleep, hundreds as one.
In the morning, I sweep their fallen feathers.
They see me staring through the window,
Eavesdropping on their chatter, but they do not deprive me
Of this sound of my old country.
In the garden overgrown, they feast daily
On fruits and beetles, seeds, and worms.
It seems my garden has much to offer them.

I feel transient next to their world of song and survival.
They have taught me to step more softly
And they cease to scatter at my approach in the garden.
The sparrows have begun to eat the fallen seeds next to me
Instead of the seeds at a distance from me.

When there are no seeds left, they take flight,
And in the old country, I would have looked on
With a jealous gaze, wishing to take flight as easily as they.
But here I am grounded, I do not wish for flight
As I have at last found my place
In this little country in the middle of the Earth.
The sparrows herald the dawn and have guided me home.

A. E. Hayoun

AGAIN

The first time, you never knew there were choices.
You were born into them, or others made them for you.
But to be reborn is to choose for yourself.
From the smallest to the largest, the choice is yours.

Where to live: in your place of birth or place of choice?
Who to befriend: those you know or someone new?
Which to love: that which is near
Or that which you must discover?
What to eat: the familiar or the foreign?

Will you only continue the endless labor of yearning
Or will you work to fulfill your desire of old?
Where do you find your joy,
From what is given to you or from what you create?
How will you keep yourself,
In familiar comfort or in wild courage?

Will your year just take you once again around the sun
Or on a great journey?
More than we know, we determine when it is our time
To root, blossom, and grow.

I am born again unto the land I love.
I am trading English for Hebrew, squirrels for cats,
Intersections for roundabouts,
A pound of this for a kilo of that.
I am beginning again.

WRITER ON THE ROOF

"O what a melancholy choice this is"
Being home
Wanting home
Taking myself from the people whom I know
Building the home I love.
This is where my heart has settled long ago
I am here
I can't go.
Who could imagine I'd be mourning so
Far from family I love
Yet
Here in my home
I love.

Ode to "Far from the Home I Love" from Fiddler on the Roof

A. E. Hayoun

Garden

In the garden entrusted to my care,
I weed, water, and prune away the old and useless,
Revealing new growth and fresh perspective.
Nourishing fruits and delicious shade
Are my full payment in return.
Every day, the weeds return as proof
Of the life within my garden.
The birds revel in the thorns and thistles,
And bugs gather at their stalks,
I take care to leave a portion
For their pleasure as well as my own.
Birds bathe in the dust under the trees
And cats prowl in hedges.
A garden in the desert is a garden for all.

At midday, lizards and beetles, cats, and birds alike
Find shared ground and common shade,
Anywhere to escape the burning sun
Under which the lemon trees flourish.
As I dig shallow holes for new vines,
My mind turns toward the ground,
Wondering what ancient treasures are buried below
And who traveled on this land when the Judges ruled.

When it first became mine,
I thought I was caring for my garden,
But I am beginning to realize
That my garden is caring for me.
It brings me out into the light, gifting me flowers and herbs.
Day after day I tend the garden and it is I who flourish.
I walk with bare feet and rest in the shade of the pear tree.
Lying in the dust, how could I have forgotten?
The pleasures of the earth, the heat of the sun
Well-known in childhood,
But easily forgotten once we are grown.
I have returned to the joys of arboreal shade
And sunburned arms tired from digging.

The Camel in the Forest

To the north at the garden's edge is a stone wall
Trellising passionfruit and an old grapevine.
The stacked stones are the face of an old woman
Looking out from behind her long hair of vines.
She is bedecked in flowers, bees, and ancient grapes.
She watches me grow my garden and into my new life.
I arrange her viney tresses and trim away the old
So new green can frame her face.

By night she perspires dew of the moon,
At dawn she softens in new light,
And in that same new light I wake
And robe myself in fronds and fruit, lemons, and lavender.
I am Hava returned, the Jewess in her garden,
A queen in the Negev, wrapped in fig leaves
And almonds, grape leaves and wheat,
Rooting deeply into a new life in my garden.

A. E. Hayoun

KITCHEN

In the kitchen I knew. In the kitchen I know.
Cilantro is coriander, in Hebrew, cusbara.
Garlic does not come in heads
But by the teeth, *shen shel shum*.
The transition from salsa to harisa is not at all unwelcome.
The dafna of Mediterranean kings
Has a different flavor from the bay leaf I know.
The cumin here is whole and tastes of a world of flavors.
The king of the table are the eggplants;
Four types of hatzilim are arrayed on the table.
At his side, his queen is spicy matbucha bedecked in garlic,
Made from tomatoes that blush year 'round.

Glistening in olive oil from groves not far from my home,
Everything shimmers in shemin zayit.
Baharat and hawaij, brought home with the exiled,
Enliven soups and those ubiquitous kitzitzot.
Za'atar and hummus are served with daily bread.
Hel and Amba from India and Baghdadi Bombay
Season strong coffee and street shawarma.

I am invited to enter the kitchens of the women,
The mothers and aunts, sisters, and cousins, where
They speak Hebrew, Spanish, and al-Arabiya diyalna.
Though I bring my English and a dash of Hebrew,
We communicate through the food we prepare.
Peeling lentils, washing fennel,
Shaping levivot, and rolling out dough.
On the table are red wine and mafrum,
Eleven salatim in their shining bowls.
Women eagerly push pieces
Of orange juice-soaked coconut cake into my mouth,
Saying, "*Titami*, I made this especially for you."
They press chewy sesame and honey bites into my hands,
And they place endless fried kishu onto my plate.

Shabbat mornings, the family is together

The Camel in the Forest

Preparing trays ladened with breakfast,
There are lemon preserves, whipped avocado, fresh eggs,
Toasted challah, bowls of cafe, and chocolate babka.
Marinated cucumbers sit next to bowls of olives
Salty fish, and a fresh fruit salad.
In the winter and spring,
Oh, the glasses of fresh citrus juice!
Pomelo, eshkoliot, and tapuz.

Once the Shabbat queen departs,
I return to my home with nutcakes soaked in honey water
To eat with nana tea or cafe shahor.
I return to my kitchen with the lingering flavors
Of fresh cream puffs and delicious vegetables in my mouth.
I turn to my own vegetables with fresh perspective
And prepare them according to the memory of taste.
Couscous, Nile perch in tangy chraime sauce,
And green garlicky mujdei to eat with everything.

In a beautiful evolution of cooking,
My hands begin to prepare a different cuisine.
Time passes and they become my salatim
Adorning the Shabbat table, and my flavors
Prepared in the kitchen I know.

A. E. Hayoun

Neighbors

To our new home in an old house,
The neighbors arrive, bearing fruits and bread,
Offering help and giving advice.
Shouting greetings, "Shalom, shalom, baruhim habaim!"

For weeks they have knocked,
And sometimes have not, to check how we are
And to give advice about life in the yishuv.
They show me their gardens and serve tea on the lawn.
They speak of their old countries,
Of the evil that drove them out,
And the decades they have spent building their lives anew
In this land of their grandparents' yearning.

As each season passes, the neighbors come with gifts:
Winter jars of olives in brine,
Springtime herbs fresh and green,
Soft summer figs swollen with juice,
And fall pomegranates for Rosh HaShana.

They watch everything change:
The house from old to renewed
And our family from newcomers to part of the yishuv.
They sweeten the transition from old house to ours anew.

LEMON

House of lemons
Growing juicy on trees
Planted in the loamy sand of the Darom,
Where I see a different set of stars
That determines the other side of the clock
When the sun will rise over Hiran
And burn down beyond Lahav
A new west, facing a new east
Where I no longer see Jerusalem
That now lies to my North
Towards the forest
Where the jackals howl at the moon
When she rises over the hills
Full of sleeping parrots and
A thick blanket of dew
That evaporates in mists
As the morning sun rises
Over ancient ruins resting
In the Negev Desert of old.

A. E. Hayoun

COMPOST

Driving out of town, towards the sea,
We drive past a great mountain of green.
Birds wheel above the lush mountain
That sticks out in the middle of the plains.
It is a beautiful sight and for a moment
I believe it is a natural mountain
Until I notice dump trucks encircling it.

"That's the mizballa, where all the trash goes."
Of all the landfills I had ever seen in other countries,
They were always at a distance.
But suddenly its different, in this tiny country,
The landfill is as close as the sea.

When I dreamed of my homeland,
I never imagined the trash,
Never thought about where it went.
Stuffed into the Holy Land,
Day after day, growing year by year.

I look at my own trash, my refuse, and scraps,
They are heavy as I take them in my hands,
Those peels and ends, scraps, and crumbs.
In a corner of the garden, I dig a deep pit
Where I lay them to rest and cover them with loam.
I turn them occasionally and wait patiently
As they transform into rich earth
That I will use to feed this land that I love so well.

PARDES

The Aleph Bet hangs like fruit from branches in my garden.
Hebrew letters, delicious on the tongue
And nourishing to the soul.
They dangle from branches high and low,
Some are easier to reach, while others reach the heavens.
They are dewy at dawn, burnished at midday,
And a joy to behold in the soft moonlight.

When I water my garden, I reach for them.
At first, my fingers touch only the lowest fruits,
The easiest sounds, but as my feet take root
And I become a part of this land,
I reach higher branches and taste richer sounds.
I practice them aloud as I prune my plants:
Samech for succulents,
Lamed for juicy lemons, and pey for tart passiflora.
The low-hanging fruits, the familiar sounds.

As I reach higher into the leafy canopy,
The sounds are like grafted fruits, familiar,
Belonging to the same sound family,
But pronounced differently.
The aleph sounds like an "h"
But weaker like avatiah, watermelon,
There is a mem for ma'arva, sage,
And gimel like soft guiava, guava.
I practice them all, rolling them inside my mouth,
Enjoying the flavor of each distinct sound.
It takes time to distinguish some sounds.
Tav at a word's end can sound like Shabbat or Shabbas,
And tet sounds like tav but is mostly used in foreign words.

As I become more established in my garden,
I whisper and sing the letters to the blossoms and the vines.
When I can reach the highest branches,
I find the resh for ripe rimon, pomegranate,
It lodges in the back of my throat

As does the ayin of anavim, grapes.
Over time my throat grows accustomed to the new
Guttural sounds like the het of hutmit, hollyhocks.

At the top of the tree, only the shamayim is above me.
I have harvested the Aleph Bet and tasted it all.
I carry the sounds in my pocket
And their flowers in my hair.
The Aleph Bet, like an abundant orchard
Of knowledge and truth, grows within me
Rooting, reaching, ripening.

ISRAELIT

I had a photograph of a girl I knew,
Not very well, she was merely an acquaintance,
But I carried her picture with me for years.

In a green plastic chair in a fluorescent-lit room,
She sat in a pink sundress, white teeth smiling with joy
Her tan hands clutching the blue cover of an Israeli ID card
With her photograph, name, and new Israeli address.

The pure joy shining in such a plain room
Shone out beyond the bounds of that photograph.
It filled me not with joy but with jealousy.
The feeling was like seeing
Your love in the arms of another.

Years passed, and with tan sandaled feet,
I now climb a Jerusalem mountain.
Strong wind blows my cotton sundress against my legs
As I climb my own Jacob's ladder.
Now I sit in a green plastic chair in a plain white room.

A silent woman staples and stacks piles of paperwork
A few hours of bureaucracy pass,
But then it is finished, and I am Israeli.
Standing next to an Israeli flag, me in my dress,
There is a photographer taking wedding pictures
Of the marriage of myself to the land I love, and it unto me.

I descend the mountain and join my people
For lunch in the Old City, a sabich b'pita.
And as if gazing down from above,
From beyond myself, I see me in Jerusalem
Radiating the true joy of love fulfilled.

A. E. Hayoun

NEGEVIM

In the grocery store, at the bank, all around me
I look at the people of the Negev.
The majority are Sephardim and Mizrahim from North Africa
West Asia, and the Arabian and Iberian peninsulas.
Though they fled Arab genocide
And the Nazis' invasion of North Africa,
They were still seen as second-class citizens
By their fellow Jews who had escaped the same evils in Europe.

As they waited for their homes to be built,
The Mizrahim were placed in tents in the Negev.
The Ashkenazim gave them the Negev
Where they believed was second best;
A home far from Tel Aviv, at a distance from Yerushalayim.

Far from culture and control,
Given land to share with the Bedouin,
To make the best until something better could be managed.
Later perhaps.
Such mistaken thinking, giving them what they believed
Was the difficult, the distant,
And the undesirable desert in Israel.
Because really the Mizrahim were given
The land of magic and power,
And therein they fostered a greater will to survive.

It has taken time, but the Negev has become
The first choice for the choicest people.
Given the choice again, between the Negev and Tel Aviv,
Most would stay in their Negev homes.
Bedouin and Mizrahim now have an understanding,
A working relationship,
Better than any other combination of people would have had.
The Bedouin speak their Arabic,
The Moroccans and Tunisians speak theirs,
And for generations, they have worked together,
Sharing Arabic, learning Hebrew,
And creating an understanding.

An understanding that now lives on in the Negev,
Jew and Bedouin, side by side, in the grocery store, at the bank
All around me, the people of the Negev.

A. E. Hayoun

CAMEL

Evening fades in from the forest,
As I stand in my garden drinking in the cold air
That blows through the trees from the north
Carrying with it scents of clean pine and heady eucalyptus.

I think about life, the one I have lived and the one I am building.
I consider both purpose and place, time, and reason,
As I am washed in the cold Negev wind.
My eyes are wide open as I watch the forest foothills
Bathed in twilight blue of the last light that cannot be seen

My eyes strain to see into the growing darkness.
But I see you there, camel in the forest,
Grazing on saltbush under a forest pine.
Tan against green, ship of the desert standing among trees.

So unusual was this twilight vision that I hold my breath,
Believing the camel would vanish if I even blinked.
A camel of the desert, an unmistakable creature
Outside of its predictable habitat, flourishing in another,
Adapting and thriving in the forest.

Out of my familiar habitat, living a life beyond what I know,
I have chosen the desert and its forests,
Where I also live, flourish, and grow
Just like the camel in the forest.

MISSING

There are the things I miss:
Year-around jalapeños, a front yard mailbox,
Phone calls in English, and my family.
The list is short, but the missing is great.

The ways you know are easier, the familiar things comforting,
But the business of life is finding yourself again in the new,
And learning to love what is different.
I may cry when I least expect it,
Over the vegetables in the market,
On the way to get my mail,
Or on birthdays without my mom,
But it passes.

I meet neighbors and new friends
In the center of the yishuv while collecting my mail.
I enjoy the flavor of the native Israeli peppers.
And my poor Hebrew is beginning to improve.

I used to straddle two worlds, but now I am comfortable in both.
And the distance to home grows shorter with each passing day.

A. E. Hayoun

SHUK

You are no longer a tourist; you are an immigrant now.
You may not feel ready to experience the shuk alone,
But there is no other way than trial by fire, sink or swim,
To the shuk on your own.
Forget the immigration office,
The shuk is where you test your immigrant mettle,
Where you raise yourself to the Israeli challenge.

You have practiced your vocabulary words,
You brought your national ID in case someone asks to see it
(no one will).
Shopping list in hand and you are ready.
You step off the bus into the shady
Corridors of the Old City shuk.
You feel confident and prepared, but you still have your doubts.
You can imitate the sabra swagger but the façade is gone
When you jump away in fright from the man at the halva stall,
His knife raised as he yells out flavors with the fervor
Of a revolutionist at a protest, "Chocolate, pistachio, vanilla!"
You pass him, calm down, and with fists clenched
You set out determined to buy everything on your list
And then reward your bravery with a cafe v'maafe.

Pushing through shouting crowds, past yelling vendors,
The paper in your hand starts to feel
More like a battle plan than a grocery list.
The first order of business: bread.
Down the long corridor of stalls, you smell a bakery,
Walking closer you see that there are three:
One screaming in Arabic,
Another sleeping in Hebrew,
And the third managed by a young boy doling out pastries
And counting change at the speed of a mixer set on high.
As you approach the third, you realize
That the line of people stretching
Down the length of the shuk corridor is the line for the third bakery.
Your stomach is not up for the wait,

The Camel in the Forest

Nor is your confidence up to fighting for your place in line.
You avoid confrontation with the screamer
And decide to awaken the sleeper.
With a snort and a drag on an unlit cigarette,
The large man wordlessly starts bagging bread and pastries,
Possibly including the ones you asked for.
You open your mouth to protest
The additional unsolicited baked goods in your bag,
But before you get a word out,
The cigarette starts wagging and you hear,
"It's on the house. Welcome to Izrael."
With a wink, he presses brass coins into your hand
And you are off on your next mission.

Some reconnaissance is necessary
Before you begin approaching stalls.
The stall with the vegetables most beautifully
On display is often the most expensive,
The prices support the swarthy stall owner
Who is also on display.
Stroking his produce, he calls out for you to buy his wares.
Save your shekels and continue your way.
There are the screamers of varying ethnicities,
United in their fervor,
But they are more intent on outscreaming the other
Than selling their wares to you.
There is the Hasidic man and his sons on one side,
They chat with the local bubbes who know them by name.
Across from them, there is a sweet saba
Standing behind his shining produce,
He is unaware of where he is much less
That he is manning his produce stall.
If you approach, you will receive
A bouquet of winks and a gummy smile,
But a handsome young grandson
Will come from the back of the stall
To take your order and count your change.

You have made it this far, and now you need eggs.
You have gained some confidence
And you are feeling more prepared,
Until you reach the stall that sells eggs.

Sold by the same woman who sells cheeses;
The eggs, oh, the eggs.
Your turn in line comes and you find yourself staring
At a large soft drink refrigerator
With stacks of egg cartons inside.
The refrigerator has no door
And the electrical cable is lying on the floor
Nowhere near an electrical outlet.
Food safety warnings and visions
Of salmonella poisoning flash before your eyes.
Standing at the front of the line now,
You are just staring at cartons of warm eggs.
The stall owner says without question,
"At lo mipo." "You're not from here."
Your national ID blazes in your pocket,
New as the pink ID stamped onto each egg,
But you keep its existence to yourself
And instead like the simple son at the Pesach table,
You ask, "What makes these eggs different from all other eggs
that they can be kept unrefrigerated in the desert?"
The woman at the stall stares incredulously at you
As you stare incredulously at the eggs.
Selecting a carton of eggs, unwashed of their mother's fluids,
Dotted with downy feathers, she thrusts them into your arms
And says, "Eggs are not washed; they don't have to be cold."
She takes your money and with your change
She gives you a piece of cheese to try.
Eyebrows cocked, she waits for you to finish chewing,
"Now you'll buy some for your bread."
The cheese is so delicious there is no argument to broach.
She selects a block of bulgarit
And a large container of goat cheese.
"When you come to shuk, you bring basket."
She instructs you in broken English
Better than your broken Hebrew.

A delicious meal has taken shape
In the bags hanging from your arms
And the moment has arrived
To reward your efforts with a coffee.
The search begins for great coffee, the national pastime,
The fuel that fires the entire country.

The Camel in the Forest

Every man sitting on a stool outside their stall
Has a cup of coffee in hand.
Bedouin men sit in the nargila lounge at the edge of the shuk
Where smoke billows out under the awning
As they sip tiny cups of black coffee with hel.
Most stalls in the shuk sell coffee from large espresso machines
Balanced precariously on tiny shelves
Next to the cash register and tzedaka boxes.
From the bakery to the meat stall,
Anyone in the shuk will sell you a cup of coffee,
But if you want a good coffee, never ask at those stalls
Or theirs will surely be the best,
"The finest coffee in the Middle East!"
Rather, ask at a stall that does not sell coffee
And you will usually be directed to the spice stall.

You will smell the spice stall before you see it.
Managed by a young Bedouin man, spices, kasher badatz,
Are arranged in towering pyramids.
The spice stall's espresso machine also sits precariously
Next to the cash register on a too-narrow shelf
But the spice stall has the largest variety
Of different coffee beans and various grinds.
You ask him to serve what he recommends,
Which he brews and pours into a brown paper cup.
Dark roasted coffee with hel and a little sugar,
Delicious and invigorating.
He takes you on a tour of his spices,
As proud as a father of his children.
There is no way to leave the spice stall
Without a few new spices in hand wrapped in little paper bags.

With your coffee in hand, you sit in the sun
On a stone wall at the edge of the shuk.
As you enjoy your spoils of war,
You watch the bustle of Israelis pass by.
You have survived the shuk and are ready to join their ranks.
But next time you should bring a basket.

A. E. Hayoun

HUTZPA

Call it hutzpa, rudeness, or audacity,
But it is that Israeli confidence that keeps this country running.
The ability to ask until they receive, and if they don't,
To ask again until they do.

Ingrained within them from the day they are born,
They know nothing is for free,
No one owes you anything,
And you must ask for everything.

In Israel, there are no signs stating,
"If you see something, say something"
Because Israelis cannot stop themselves from saying anything
And getting involved in everything.

In a country of lions, I often feel like a cub,
Born with the same abilities but still learning how to use them.
To not only have a voice but to know how to use it.
And use it in my second language.

In a country that gets right to the point,
I am learning to skip the pleasantries,
Drop the smile and raise my voice, and if necessary,
Raise it louder than the rest.
And like the rest, I am learning how to help,
No matter who and no matter the circumstances.

You may not always want them
In your personal space or private life
But in a society of Israelis, you will never
Have to guess what anyone is thinking.
And it is because of all this hutzpa
That this country was decolonized,
Our dead language revived, and our homeland revitalized.

But it's still hutzpa baby steps for me:
Keeping my place in line at the post office,

The Camel in the Forest

Calling to make appointments in Hebrew.
Hutzpa doesn't come naturally to an American,
But like everything else, hutzpa comes with practice.

A. E. Hayoun

WINE

From the land of amphorae and wineskins,
Wine was transported on wooden ships
From ancient Israel to the Roman Empire.
From this land to Europe and beyond,
The first vines were brought from
The regions of Kna'an, the Negev, and the Galil.

Ancient vineyards, lost to exile and destruction,
Have been joyously replanted.
Grapevines flourish in the desert in old Nabatean terraces
And take root beside the ancient wine presses of Yatir.
Chewable wines in reds and purples,
Summer wines of gold and green.

From the vines of antiquity, we drink the grapes' juice
Of shiraz, chardonnay, and rich muscat.
A land rich in viticulture, ancient vineyards,
And biblical wine-drinking.
We may have swapped wineskins for glass stems
But we have returned to our vines.

PETIT PAYS

Your star is the spark
That ignites your people.

From the sea to the desert
They rest in your cradle.

From across the world,
They come into your arms.

Small country, full of magic
In the Golan, in the Negev.

Ancient country, full of love
For the Temple, for their right hands.

Such great longing, thousands of years.
Oh, that ancient yearning, now fulfilled.

Petit pays, je t'aime beaucoup
Petit petit, je l'aime beaucoup

Ode to "Petit Pays" by Cesária Evora

EXCAVATION

Sharing a ride into town, on the way to Be'er Sheva,
Great black tents rise up on the right like small canvas hills.
Whizzing quickly past, craning my neck,
I see great cuts into the earth
Like short stairs downwards into a narrow ditch full of people
Wearing large-brimmed hats, wielding
Small brushes and little trowels.

"They found some ancient ruins
While digging out the site for the new bus stop.
So they have stopped construction to excavate them.
It's a nuisance really, slowing traffic and delaying the project."
Said the driver absentmindedly.
What a nuisance it must be to have a mind that lacks wonder,
A mind that cannot marvel at such a gift, I thought.
A gift of the ancient, of the secret and hidden,
Unexpectedly revealed.

The gift of an opportunity to discover the undiscovered.
The gift of meeting the unknown,
Of learning more about who came before
So we can learn more about who we are now.
I had never experienced this type of wonder,
Other types of wonder, yes, but not one so ancient and special.

On the return home from Be'er Sheva,
I asked to pull over at the old bus stop,
A short distance from the site of the new.
Walking towards the now-empty canvas tents
Lit by the setting sun, I peered into the excavation site
And saw scattered ancient stones, neither floor nor wall,
Just stone lying about as though discarded.
I saw the steps cut into the earth by the archaeologists,
The brush strokes of painstakingly slow
Brushing away of sand and loam,
Cutting and brushing step by step into the earth
To gently reveal some ancient wonder.

The Camel in the Forest

Back in the vehicle, driving on the highway,
Something had changed for me.
The ground I walked on was now
A sort of hallowed I had not yet known.
Not hallowed of the divine but hallowed of the people.
Every step above ground was over a piece of the ancient past.

Months passed, they paved over the site
And established the new bus stop.
I heard tell that it was not a "real" archaeological site,
But just a few carved stones left behind
By ancient builders or destructive marauders.
The stones had been cataloged and removed, the bus stop built,
And the traffic of life continued ever onwards.

A. E. Hayoun

MALKA

From the shade of a palm tree, I watch the woman in the shuk.
Her strong hands pull a woven basket
And seek out the ripest tomatoes.
Fingers point to the choicest cuts,
Eyes follow swift hands counting change,
Her nose detects the ripest strawberries,
And her experienced tongue haggles.

Shouts from the left and right do not deter her,
She wavers not from her course.
Her feet follow a familiar path over the uneven stone floor,
Around puddles and squashed produce
To the stalls where she is known.
"Shalom, giveret, mah shlomech?"

She holds her list in her mind.
A strong back pulls her heavy basket
That is full of goat cheese, shiny eggplants,
Fennel, and a kilo of beans.
For her family, she cooks what she loves
And they love what she cooks.
She never doubts her ingredients or their best season.
Confident in her abilities, she needs no help,
But she will always ask the fishmonger,
"Which catch is the freshest?"
And to the baker, "Which loaves are fresh from the oven?"

Her tomatoes adore her, they flush at her touch,
Onions do not make her weep,
And peppers do not burn her hands.
For her, beans shed their skins gladly,
And the dates loosen their pits.
Rice washes itself, and insects abandon her lettuce.
The shuk is her kingdom and the produce her subjects.
Though her rule is absolute, she is benevolent and wise.

In her kitchen, utensils stand to attention,
And on her table, her dishes are recumbent before her.

The Camel in the Forest

Vegetables bask in her seasonings,
Fruits gleam in beautiful pottery on her clean wooden table.
Her food scraps are honored, given a place in her compost,
Where they transform from rot to black gold,
To feed her fruit trees and nourish her garden.

The woman in the shuk is a queen in her kitchen.
Resting now in the shade of the palm tree, I watch
And wonder, how many trips to the shuk until I become queen?

A. E. Hayoun

SHABBAT

It comes and it goes, it begins when it ends.
Eternal Shabbat, ever new. Shabbat Havdalah Shabbat.

Yom Rishon
Life and home are returned to their yom hol state.
Thoughts still linger on the holy, time of togetherness and rest,
The delicious food that was, and the week that lies ahead.

Yom Sheni
Anticipation of the next Shabbat hangs in the air
Like the lingering scent in the kitchen
Of the freshly baked challah devoured over Shabbat.

Yom Shlishi
Lists are written, plans arranged,
And visitors are invited to celebrate together,
Bezrat HaShem, the upcoming Shabbat.

Yom Revi'i
Arrangements are made, plans are finalized.
Comestibles and vegetables,
Wine and treats are purchased and sorted.

Yom Hamishi
The excitement builds, the cooking commences.
And all the houses are shaken out.
The week is behind, Shabbat ahead.

Yom Shishi
The air in Israel is electric, fragrant, and golden
With anticipation of the Shabbat queen's arrival.
Even for those who do not keep it,
The feeling of Shabbat is in the air.

The great table is set with silver and linens.
Dishes are prepared with special thoughts
For honoring HaShem and the Shabbat,
His weekly gift to the Jews.

The Camel in the Forest

Returned from ritual baths, dressed in finery,
A blessing is sung before candlelight.
The mystical poetry of Shlomo is recited
To escort the Shabbat queen and her angels into each home.

The men sing a song
For the women and the torat-chesed on their tongues.
Sons are blessed as Ephraim and Menashe,
Daughters endowed with the power of the matriarchs.

Wine is poured and blessed.
Hands are washed and silence reigns
As the challah is raised, blessed, sliced, and salted.
An "Amen" and the meal begins.

A banquet of beauty and delight stretches the length of the table.
All are nourished, body and soul. Peace pervades.

Yom Shabbat
We rest and repeat,
Waiting for the eternal Shabbat with The Divine Creator
In Whom we rest.
In the meantime, "l'chaim!" and have some more wine,
Tonight it ends and tomorrow it begins.

A. E. Hayoun

TAVOR

Walking through town, riding the bus,
At the beach, or sitting at the next table,
The young soldiers carry their assault rifles everywhere they go.

Warriors, both male and female,
Join combat units to defend their country,
The land of their parents, grandparents, and ancestors.
At eighteen or nineteen, they are ready for battle,
To fight any threat to their people and their land.

Combat soldiers on leave,
Dressed in shorts and a t-shirt, flip-flops or sandals,
But always the Tavor-21 slung at their side.
That compulsory weight they can never leave behind.

Until one day, a few years later, it will be their last day to serve,
And they will be free to return to their homes as civilians
In the land they fought for,
In Israel, the land of their birthright.

BINOCULARS

A gift for gazing at moon craters and distant stars,
A present for looking, forward and beyond,
With lenses to see what the distance hides from my eyes.

In the evenings, I gaze at the celestial beauties,
Loving them more upon closer inspection,
But my vision wanders, and I begin to look closer to earth.

By day I gaze over the wall of the courtyard and beyond.
Into the expanse of desert, seemingly empty before,
Now with keener sight, I see it is teeming with life.

Sweeping dunes and rocky ruins,
Camels grazing on imperceptible nourishment.
Bedouin on horses, both with headdresses,
Vultures and crows swooping and feasting.

Along the horizon, in every direction,
Tall hills and low mountains stand out like beacons.
The closest forest has towering eucalyptus trees
Growing next to wind-blown pines,
Both are home to the nests of Negev birds.

The binoculars brought the distance closer,
Details to life, and a yearning for adventure.
What am I searching for with my binoculars?
Something in the distance? Something more?

DANCE

I love more deeply than ever I thought possible.
This land, this country, this place, my home.
I notice everything,
Like a new mother or a young lover.
The sound of the wind through the palm trees,
As enchanting to me as it was to Shlomo HaMelech.
Who so enchanted did name the sound: *Shirat HaDekel*.
Like silver in the wind is the dekel's song.

Morning dew waters my feet.
Southern sunlight darkens my arms.
Crows caw at my window, I hear the orvani's song.
Reflective sands gild my hair.
For magic sunrises, I forfeit my sleep.
Fruit blossoms scent my garden and my skin.
The bouquet of my garden changes with the seasons.
The tzufit flits from flower to flower and my soul takes flight.
These treasures of the earth, these gifts from shamayim.
All that we cannot own, all that dances before us,
To dance on forevermore.

CONTRARY

In this tiny land, in the middle of the Earth,
Contradictions abound.
Country of the contrary.
Contrary to public opinion,
Contrary to expectations,
Contrary to lies and propaganda.

Time passes and I look deeper,
With my eyes wide open and my mind receptive.
I see the truth of this utterly imperfect,
Beautifully captivating country.
Time passes and all the assumptions and preconceived notions,
Everything the world says about Israel fades,
And all that remains is the truth of lived experience.

Of apartheid, there is none, only Jews and Arabs,
Christians, Druze, and many others
Living side by side throughout the country,
Creating a considerable amount of peace in the Middle East.

In Israel, a sense of safety persists,
At night, out walking, as a woman;
A sense of safety I have never experienced
Anywhere else in the world.

And there is the daily feeling of the miraculous.
The miracle of watching the Jewish people
Thrive in their homeland.
A miracle because, by all logic,
After all the obstacles Jews have faced,
We should still be in galut,
Waiting in the golah, for our homeland.
It is all this that makes this little country unique in the world,
The miracles, the magic, and the juxtaposition of life in Israel.

A. E. Hayoun

JOURNEY

As I sit in the sunshine
Eating falafel across from the well
That Avraham purchased.
The first of many wells
That would become Be'er Sheva.
I think of the arrival of Shabbat
A few days from now.
Of parashat Vayachi
And Yosef's journey across the Sinai,
Through Be'er Sheva,
Where he too rested at this well
Before continuing his way north,
Passing my home
On the way to Hevron
To rebury the bones of his father,
Avinu Ya'akov.
Be'er Sheva is now a modern city,
But some things will never change.
Yosef will pass this way again
This coming Shabbat,
As he does every year,
In parashat Vayachi.

NIGHT

Night in the Negev, the desert is purple.
Twilight animals awaken.
Silence, save for the dukhifat
Who cries so forlornly in the night sky.

The last veil falls to reveal the stars
Twinkling and bright, ever watching.
Eternal stars that flicker in the afternoon heat
And blaze alongside the sun
Behind a veil of daytime cloud.

Under the summer Levana,
I drink herbs and flowers
And bathe in her glow,
Watching her cycles and counting my own.

The jackals' howl is sharper in winter.
Winter when the stars pierce the veil between us,
And the cold sky sits heavier on the earth.

The sands shift and the winds blow across
The secret darkness of ancient desert nights.
I sleep in my now-familiar bed,
And I will wake to another dawn in the Negev.

DESERT

Washing myself with grains of sand, gathering back pieces of time

A. E. Hayoun

FOREST

There is a mountain of boxes in our new home near the forest.
There is much to be done, but it must wait,
I have waited long enough to go exploring.
I push my feet into familiar boots and set out.
Walking between houses, under a tunnel of twisted cacti,
I pass the yishuv boundary and cross into dune and desert.

Ascending the foothills, I stand at the gates of the forest
And wait for answers to all my questions.
I hear no answer, only the orvani
Calling from within the trees.
In answer to his call, I enter the forest.
Passing ancient dolomite and crushing fragrant eucalyptus,
I walk quietly and attune my ears to the sounds of the forest.
Rocks call out to me and birds circle overhead,
Trees hum deeper as I brush past them.
The sleeping jackals continue their slumber,
Hedgehogs wake not for my passing feet.
The shifting eyes of the sunning lizard
Watch as I climb upwards past his hidden den.

Further into the forest, carried by winds that catch my breath,
The trees ahead of me grow sparser,
I have reached the top and there is no higher to climb.
Standing on a limestone plateau deep in the forest,
I face southward and look towards home.
Beyond the yishuv is an expanse of deep desert,
The beginning of the descent to the lowest point on Earth.
I have forgotten my questions and why I asked them.
Standing in the forest, wind whistling through the branches,
I find no answers, only a reason to stay.

KAN

Where is this home of mine?
Where do I plant my feet and weed my soul?
On what earth do I find myself
And seek out the view that tells me more?

Between the allocations given to Shimon and Yehuda,
There is a home in that desert where I live and breathe.
Climbing the nearest high place, my eyes can see
King David's route from Ziklag to the River Bsor.

From my garden, straight South, I could walk the Negev,
Follow the remnants of the incense route towards Mamshit,
On to Petra then return through Avdat,
Back to Aza and the Tihon Sea.

All the while, I would drink from the craters
And swim in the endless sky,
Sleep beside the ruins that have waited centuries to hold me.
Holding to my breast broken fragments of time,
As I return to my home in the Negev desert.

A. E. Hayoun

Underground

Beneath the Negev,
Under my feet,
Lie wonders of wonders
Hidden both shallow and deep.

Remnants of humans and the lives they lived
Covered and uncovered and covered again,
Folded into the ground by magma and rain.
My boots press into the Earth
Above Sheol, Arka, and Gan Eden.

Walking the desert, knowing the forest,
I rest on boulders, each a piece of time
Left over from the time before
When the wonders lived above ground,
And our feet could easily find
Adam at the entrance to paradise hidden.

CHOSEN

Have we chosen the land or has it chosen us?
Where we live lives within us,
Where we settle, settles us.
And where do I live but on earth in heaven?
Near the bottom of the world where the great rains gather.

Dwelling on high in the Dar Rum,
Between Shfalim and Yam Suf,
In this chosen land.

The southern sun climbs higher,
Dune and mountain sink lower
Over Earth's deepest hollow, the desert salt sea.
The Negev of old, the home we choose.
From exile we are returned, the Israelites, the Jews.

A. E. Hayoun

RISHONOT

Six large mouths gape open in the earth.
Six cave dwellings hidden in a hill, hidden in plain sight.
Invisible at a distance, the caves can only be seen
When standing on the hill above them.
Caves that hollow out an entire hill
Were once home to an ancient desert community.

I approached them quietly, slowly.
Admiring the ancient stone lintel of each doorway,
Still standing timelessly amongst fallen stones,
Each uniquely carved with delicate motifs.
There was no sign nearby to identify those ruins
Or signify their age, these caves were abandoned,
But not untouched.

Plastic litter and empty cans were scattered across the hill,
Among them was an abundance of ancient pottery.
Shards of history, large and small, lying exposed in the dust.
After crawling over fallen stones and crushing dry grasses,
At the entrance to each cave, I tossed in a rock and waited
For a reply from any foxes or other cave inhabitants
To make themselves known before I entered.

Some caves were small but most were large,
Deep and wide enough to be divided into rooms
Or areas to keep livestock enclosed at night.
Ancient stones covered the caves' interior
And modern trash littered the damp floor,
The cave walls and ceiling of natural limestone
Were blackened and covered in etchings.
I searched for a message, a name, or an inscription
Something to tell me who had lived in these caves,
But the cuts were only made to shape the limestone interior.
So, all that is left of the cave dwellers who were
Is the pottery they crafted and the lintels they carved.

I stayed inside until I could breathe the dampness no more.
I left the caves reluctantly, but I knew I would return.
Walking home laden with pottery shards,

The Camel in the Forest

I was determined to find a historical mention of the caves.
But I found nothing, no record was ever written
Nor were they marked on any map.
So, I gave them a name, Ma'arot HaRishonot, The First Caves.
Because they were the first I ever found exploring the Negev.

I have returned to them, time and again,
To clean up the litter and collect more pottery shards,
All the while, imagining and remembering
The people who established the caves as their home.
I have found you and I return to you.
I gave you a name and write of you here,
So that now you have a history
And a name to be remembered by.

A. E. Hayoun

EVANIM

Rock and stone,
Stacked and scattered.
For building,
For stoning,
For fire igniting.

Under twisted root,
Grounded on grassy ridge,
Strewn across field and dune,
Marking ancient vineyards.

The rocks surround me reminding me of transience,
Reminding me that they will remain long after I have passed.
They press into the earth holding down its mantle,
Keeping us from floating off into the heavens to orbit
Among the stars with the other rocks that have broken free.

Desert rocks tell me their stories.
I bring them home and they weigh me down,
Keeping me here just a little longer
Until I am ready to take my celestial flight.

FURNACE

I dig through sand and loam like the Negev hadaf
Trying to return to the deepest layers of the desert.
I wander at a snail's pace, searching the Negev
For signs of ancient life.
I look for answers in the hundreds of shards
That weigh heavily in the canvas bag at my waist.
Pieces of broken jars, bowls, and lamps all with a story,
Not a single piece escapes my sun-blind gaze.

In the shade of a virile carob tree,
I stretch myself at length like the long-extinct bardelas
Resting from the afternoon sun.
I look out to the horizon from Lahav to Hiran
And I see them, alone and at ease in the midday sun.
Tall shaggy humps, tan and brown, long spindly legs,
Striding slowly through scorching summer dunes.
Creatures of unmistakable form, camels by no other name.
Their strange beauty and singular disposition
Pair well with their home of dust plumes and windy heat.
They are indivisible from their environment of arid furnace,
And yet, their unique presence catches my eye.

Sitting in the dry heat and watching them,
Their peaceful grazing and quiet living fill me with joy.
Before I lived in the desert, camels were distant creatures,
But now I have joined them in their fiery world,
In this Negev of hot sand and sunburnt forest,
Where I share both sun and shade
With the camels in the desert.

A. E. Hayoun

POTTERY

Trails of all kinds trace their way through the desert:
Goat trails, bike trails, and hiking trails.
My feet weave their own trail on the loom of the land.
Threading my way through valleys of hard-packed earth,
Where plants bloom and are nourished by unseen waters.

In desert valleys where rustling lizards catch beetles,
And those universal flies swarm in abundance.
Where wind-blown trash has collected
And the dredges of last year's run-off have piled up.
Plastic rests in bushes and nestles devilishly between rocks,
Scattered so widely, it is impossible to gather it all back.
The plastic we use so quickly
And just as quickly turn into refuse,
The paper waste is more forgivable,
Flapping exhaustedly in the wind,
It shows signs of deterioration and its impending decay.

With each gust of wind funneled through the dry valley,
Billions of sand granules shift and jump in sun-lit wind
Bouncing over the silent rocks that bring me great joy.
Pieces of chert in mauve and taupe,
Quartz conglomerate and iron ore lie in the valley
Next to volcanic scoria so incongruous in the desert.
The limestone is the same that gives 'way to time
For the creation of the caves that lay open-mouthed
Across the Judean desert and Negev mountains.

The pottery is earthen and dusty like the rocks,
But even broken into shards it is more symmetric and human.
I gently scrape packed earth to prise out pottery shards,
And marvel at their unique designs and variety of shapes.
On one large, curved handle of an erstwhile jug,
Pressed into the clay and baked thousands of years ago,
The potter left an ancient fingerprint.
My latter-day fingers slip into the curve of the handle
As I imagine the complete jug and the person who fired it.
I sit for a while amongst the salt plants,
As the sun beats down on my back and flies tickle my skin,

The Camel in the Forest

Thinking about what the jug once held:
Wine, water, grains, or remains?

I follow the salt plants through the deep dry valley,
Picking up each piece of antiquity along the way,
Pieces of another time, remnants of humanity.
As I reach the forest, long shadows fall over the valley.
With my pockets full of pottery, I think all the while,
How it has survived for millennia so exposed to the elements,
Unless it was with great resolve to be found again.

A. E. Hayoun

LAMBS

It is spring and the Negev is changed.
Every aspect of it is unexpected; more grass than sand,
And more flowers than sandstorms.
Local birds share branches with migrating birds.
Winds blow in great gusts up from the south.
The desert has turned green as far as the eye can see.

Spring in the Negev and new life abounds:
Butterflies from their golems, chicks from their nests,
Flowers from their buds, and babies from their mothers.
Red kits and camel calves, tiny fuzzy jackal cubs,
Lambs white and pink, and soft-bristled hedgehoglets.

All this beauty spreads out before me,
Like a banquet for my senses.
In every spare moment I can find, I fly from the house
To be a part of it, of the great awakening in the desert.

I walk to the camels and praise the mothers their calves,
Tall and gangly, wobbly, and thirsty.
A large milk duct throbs along the length of the mother camel,
Professing the season of abundance.
The birds fly in great flocks, their chicks are fluffy and loud.
It is a joy to watch them being fed beetles at dawn.

To see the lambs, you must first find the herd.
Watched over by Bedouin shepherds,
The herds are either out grazing in the mornings
Or resting in the forest at midday,
Alongside the shepherds who also rest in the shade.

Find the shepherd and greet him warmly.
Ask about his year, if the grasses are plentiful for his flocks,
And then ask to see the lambs.
He might smile a small smile,
And then part slightly his robes or open his jacket
To reveal a soft lamb sleeping in the folds.
The lambs, all pink skin and white fuzz,
Are carried while they are young so as not to slow

The Camel in the Forest

The grazing herd or deter their mothers from eating
The short-lived grasses that nourish their milk.

If you ask, the shepherd might let you hold one of the lambs,
An experience you will never forget.
It is like the feeling of springtime in the desert,
And new life in the Negev.

A. E. Hayoun

GIVAT OGER

Walking in the forest, I follow a narrow and dusty trail.
Between pine and eucalyptus, I climb upwards
Through gullies and slide sideways down ridges.
In a clearing in the forest there is an old stone wall.
Toppled by time, the wall is low to the ground
And ancient stones lay scattered around it.
In the distance, at the top of the hill, I see more stones,
Not scattered but standing, a wall and cornerstones.

At the top of the hill sits the large ruins of an ancient estate,
All its previous grandeur is diminished
But the memory of wealth remains.
The ruin is the outline of an ancient many-roomed stone house
Overlooking a desert valley facing South.
There are deep cuts into the limestone foundation,
Channels and vats, the remains of a private wine press.
A canal stretches from a treading floor to a collecting vat
Where I can imagine the trickling juice of dark grapes
Flowing downwards into the great stone vat before my feet.

Circling back to the entrance of the great house,
I pass under its now-imaginary lintel,
Long destroyed by time and man.
I enter the roofless building in which an ancient mosaic floor
Stretches the length of the largest rooms.
It is a mosaic of ocean waves and blue flowers,
Exposed to the sun and the relentless flying sand.
Designed by hands now thousands of years at rest
It is dust-covered but still vibrant and wondrous.
Someone knew, thousands of years ago,
How breathtaking ocean waves in a desert home would be.

Only a person of means could have owned such an estate,
Perfectly situated en route between Petra and the sea.
He must have traded his wine for spices,
Hosted merchants, and heard their tales
Of the deep southern desert and the Arabians beyond.

With esteemed guests, he must have shared his wines

The Camel in the Forest

That had spent years fermenting in amphorae
Within the wine caves below his great house on a hill.
Now I sit in his wine caves and wonder,
"How many more years will his caves and mosaic remain?"

A. E. Hayoun

Pocket Luggage

The pocket luggage I carry with me.
Pieces of pottery, crushed eucalyptus leaves,
And found plastic gathered back.
They all take up space in my pockets that I give willingly.

I have empty pockets in the morning, by noon they begin to fill,
Come evening, I turn out their contents and sort it all away:
Pottery into boxes, leaves to the compost,
And the infamous plastic into the great blue bin.

I know little of empty pockets,
Most days, mine are carrying a world of small things.
Empty pockets reflect a lack of earthward vision,
Of endless searching for what lies forgotten on the ground,
A lack of belief in lost treasures waiting to be found.

Watch where you tread, they are there at your feet,
Shards of magic and hidden treasure,
Those long-forgotten pieces of the Great Story.

The Camel in the Forest

SULIEMAN

I saw Sulieman's sheep before I saw his tent.
Herded by large dogs, a son, and two grandsons.
On the path with my husband and hami,
We passed the herd of sheep with their jangly bells,
They were returning to Suleiman's tents.
The grandsons smiled hesitantly
And the men greeted each other formally
As the sheep continued bleating and jostling to be first.

The canvas sides of Sulieman's tent billowed outwards
As a strong wind, still cool from the last of winter,
Blew over the ridge where Sulieman had made camp.
In the winter, the ridge is empty, but as spring approaches,
Sulieman begins to graze his flocks.
I stopped to pet some beautiful many-colored goats,
Their rectangular eyes stared at me unblinkingly.
More grandsons were "burring" and "clicking" at the herd,
Urging them out into the fields.

It was a pastoral sight of the timeless shepherding trade.
Following the trail, I joined the rest at Suleiman's tent.
Three canvas sides were closed to the cold north wind
The fourth side was open, revealing a stack of mattresses,
A simple fire pit, and in the far corner of the tent
Was a not-so-small black and white heifer calf
Standing immobile and chewing peacefully.

Suleiman stood at the entrance to this tent in a cotton thob,
His red and white keffiyeh perched on his shaved head,
And thick white bristles encircled his sun-browned face.
He called out loudly to hami,
"Salaam elekum! Ahlan w'sahlan." Hello and welcome.
My father-in-law shouted back his reply in Arabic,
"Al alekum salaam, ismi..."
I had never heard my husband's father speak Arabic before.
We approached the tent and Suleiman extended
His hand outwards in a sweeping motion towards his tent
Where he and hami continued their very small talk.

A. E. Hayoun

When my father-in-law ran out of his Arabic,
Suleiman switched to Hebrew and offered us coffee.
He motioned toward his generator-powered electric kettle
On a low table beside the heifer calf, still chewing peacefully.
Suleiman told us of his early spring yield,
How many lambs and kids had been born,
And of his own offspring who helped tend his herds.
He gestured towards the pen in front of the tent
Where a squirming mass of fuzzy lambs and kids
Bleated and frolicked, butting their heads together.
Suleiman explained that he keeps the young ones
Back in the pen so their mothers can graze with the rest.

One small lamb by the fence caught my eye,
Perfectly white, wagging its short, happy tail,
The lamb was bowed low to the ground on his front legs,
Which were horribly misshapen and twisted into a knot.
The lamb propelled itself forward with its back legs
As the front legs stayed folded on the ground.
In its excitement to reach my outstretched hand,
It pushed itself towards me and nibbled at my fingers.
Suleiman watched as I stroked its fuzzy ears and twisted legs,
"He was born like that.
I tried my hardest to straighten his legs
But they are like stone.
I almost slaughtered him when he was born,
But then I saw his mother lay on the ground and turn herself
So that his mouth could reach her teat
And he could feed like the rest of the lambs.
She returns from the fields every day and runs to him,
Lying awkwardly on her side so he can eat.
For as long as she will feed him, I will not slaughter him,
But when he will be grown and no longer drink milk,
He will not be able to graze, so I will have to slaughter him."

Even in the simple seasonal lifestyle of a shepherd,
Ruled by nature's unpredictable will,
Sulieman had made room for practical sentimentality.
The she-goat and her kid would have their time together,
And when the goat was fully grown,
Suleiman would have goat's meat to feed his family.
Suleiman would never have asked us to leave,

The Camel in the Forest

But we sensed he had things to tend to.
So, we gave him our thanks for his hospitality
And made our farewells.

We followed the path back through the blooming desert
Towards the yishuv and home.
The visit to Suleiman's tent had brought me simple joy.
The heifer calf in his tent needed no explanation,
The presence of Suleiman and his offspring in the desert
Was also self-explanatory as shepherds in the Negev.
They live in tents and tend their flocks in the desert
As people have for centuries before.

A. E. Hayoun

CAVES

We never talk enough about caves.

Those magical rooms inside the Earth,
Scooped out of bedrock, cut from foundations,
Emptied and arranged like rooms
In the mansion of the universe.

The caves are full of treasures: fossils and mushrooms,
Crystals and wonders, bones and artifacts.
They are rooms of shelter and refuge,
Pockets in the globe in which we are the smallest lint.

They are surprises hidden in obscure mountain folds,
Crevices wide open in the paths before us,
Holes in the landscape, forgotten and old.

They are open to us, those mysterious caves.
They take us closer to mantle and crust,
Further from fear, nearer the core,
Into places eternal to dwell or decay.

The Camel in the Forest

HADRA

Around an unfamiliar curve, in a new part of the forest,
There was a valley in the foothills that held a meadow.
Hidden from view and lush with green.
Horses were grazing there in a small cheerful herd,
Chewing spring grasses and trotting in the afternoon sun.
Two young brown horses, a third strong black horse,
And beside me near the path was a white mare.
She stood peacefully swishing her long white tail.
My eyes drank in the beauty of this secret spring meadow,
Amazed at the contrast between the desert beyond
And this quiet pocket of green.

With silent feet and gentle breath, I approached the mare
And kneeled before her to take her picture.
At a noise on the path behind me, I froze and turned slowly,
Finding myself kneeling before six Bedouin boys.
They were all very young, only one was sixteen or so,
But the rest ranged from four- to ten-years-old.
We stared at each other for a few moments.
As they started to discuss me in Arabic,
Toothy grins began to spread across their sun-tanned faces.
I stood up and greeted them, and the youngest came forward,
Speaking to me in Arabic with the confidence of a child
Who believes his language needs no translation.
He pointed to my binoculars, chore coat, and boots
And then studied my camera and laughed at my canvas hat.
He was funny and roguishly curious, and evidently
Had not seen many like me, a woman alone in the forest.

In Hebrew, the eldest asked me, "Where are you going?"
His question assumed I was on a journey,
One with an endpoint, but in fact, I had none.
I was enjoying one of my usual forest wanderings.
While considering my answer, it became irrelevant,
As the eldest boy continued, "These are my father's horses.
We are bringing them home."
I looked from the four-year-old to the sixteen-year-old
And chuckled as I imagined them herding horses back home.

A. E. Hayoun

I asked, "Where is home?" and several tanned hands
Pointed southwest in unison and the eldest said, "Lakiya."

The youngest boys kept up their chatter about my person
And my camera while the eldest asked me,
"Do you want to take her picture? Her name is Hadra.
She is the most beautiful. You must take her picture."
Hadra the mare was beautiful, in fact, she was glowing
In the filtered afternoon light streaming through the pines.
I crouched beside her again to take her picture,
Behind me, six heads hovered over mine
And twelve eyes watched my camera.
The youngest boy giggled hot breath near my ear.
When I finished with Hadra, I turned around quickly
To face the surprised pack of boys and asked,
"Can I take your picture?" as I held my camera up to them.
The question was translated for the rest,
And suddenly they were all bashful and silent.
A boy of about ten stepped out from the group
And said in broken Hebrew, "You don't want their picture.
Just mine. I am the handsome one."
He needed no translation.
The rest of the boys giggled and shoved him.
With my camera, I captured their laughter
And the fleeting joy of boyhood in the forest.

They settled into the grass and began passing around
Bottles of soft drinks and bags of snacks.
"For you," offered the eldest boy passing me a snack bag.
I saw in the younger boys that it was reluctantly given,
Someone had been made to forfeit their snack.
I declined politely and the snack was tossed back
Into the great chorus of munching.
Minutes later, the snack bags were empty,
Carried by the wind, they began to drift over the grass.
I snatched at each bag as they floated past me,
And alone chased after the ones I had missed.
Six faces wreathed in amusement watched incredulously
As I gathered back all their trash.
Handing the empty snack bags to the eldest boy,
I told him, "Take them with you, throw them away
In a dumpster somewhere, don't let them ruin the forest."

The Camel in the Forest

Stuffing them into his backpack with a confused half-smile
He dug deeper for more snacks and returned
To the Arabic chatter that echoed around the meadow.

I began my walk back home,
Up the side of the valley towards the sunset.
I glanced back at the meadow below,
Alive with the sound of boys and horses
Living their lives on the freshness of the wind.
The same wind that swept up their plastic trash
And set it free like birds in the air
To land deeper in the forest and mar the ancient ruins.
On my way home, my eyes noticed every plastic bag,
Empty can, discarded tire, and plastic bottle.
It all lay half-buried or scattered across the forest and desert.
Unless gathered back, it would become forever
A part of the future landscape of the Negev
Long after Hadra and her boys, myself, and my words
Will have become dust of the Earth and chaff in the wind.

A. E. Hayoun

KALANIYOT

They come in droves for Darom Adom,
To frolic in and photograph
The whimsical red anemones
Of spring in the Negev.

Be careful, watch your step.
Close your hands tight.
Resist the urge to sweep them up
And let their petals take flight.
Over-picked and consequently protected
Are those vermilion corollas on spindly stems
Waving bravely under the early spring sun.

They place signs and banners to guide you
To where they want you to gather and gaze,
But hidden and many are the places to find
Anemones in abundance.

Follow the forest into valleys half-shadowed
And into meadows of low light,
There you will find carpets of blooms
That await your admiration and praise.
But they are there for only a moment,
For the duration of the brief Negev spring.

REFUSE

I want to ignore it, but the trash is everywhere.
In the forest, in the desert, filling the wadis and the wells.
Orphaned trash and abandoned plastic.
It is not what I imagined Israel would look like,
It utterly changes the wild Negev I anticipated.

There is no single perpetrator, it is a national problem
That crosses cultures and regions.
There are equal amounts of water bottles in Hebrew
And cans of tuna with labels in Arabic
Languishing in forest and desert.

As with everything else, the problem must be education.
If the trash is present in the forests and the desert
Then it must be that Israelis are not taught
About the importance of caring for nature.
Or are they aware that they need to care,
And the trash I see is only escaped wind-blown trash?

But there is too much of it in the Negev
For it to be an accident.
And where are the park rangers?
I have only ever seen them in gift shops at national parks.
Why don't they patrol the forests and the desert?
Maybe if no one is enforcing a solution,
Then no one knows that there is a problem?

Regardless of the reason, the problem belongs to all of us.
Jew and Bedouin, Druze and Arab,
Each person who calls this land their home
Must take responsibility.
The vast quantities of refuse and plastic cannot be ignored,
They are brazen in their presence across this land.

But there is a way back to the wild and it begins with us.
Changing our own habits and demanding change
From those who wield power to enforce it.
We must change for a better future and make a return,
A return to our land before the plastics.

A. E. Hayoun

NAMELESS

At the nameless horva, I found a bone.
Riddled with pockmarks, holes, and grey decay.
Once so important to the body it carried,
Once as much alive as I am now
Standing within its ancient, demolished home.

To dust we return, but slowly.
First the flesh, then the sinew, fascia, and viscera.
But the bone, how much longer does it remain?
Well after the rest has turned to dust.
Enduring centuries of change,
Of earth piling up speck by speck, year by year
Creating a unique patina of time and loss.

And this is how I found you, in your slow exhaustive state,
Ready for your honors, and honor you I do.
Bone of bandit, woman, or warrior.
I see your land, the remains of two small buildings.
Four cave dwellings on one-half dunam for your crops,
Facing east towards the foothills of the timeless Negev.

Was it enough? Did you thrive?
What did you grow and what did you eat?
Did you ever wonder about the future,
About whom might stand in your fields one day?
Just as I wonder who were you,
You who lived in these caves?

BOYS

I came upon them in a picnic area of the forest,
Two young Bedouin boys, no older than eight and eleven.
In the clearing was an ewe in the throes of labor,
Not an unusual sight in the Negev.

The two boys were passing the time talking
As they waited impatiently for the ewe to finish giving birth.
It was evident, even to my inexperienced eye,
That we were not witnesses to a normal birth.
The boys came to where I was sitting in the shade
And asked in broken Hebrew if I had any food to share.
They took my offered apple and bag of chips
And returned to sit near the ewe.

In the shade of an age-old olive tree, the ewe
Quivered and struggled as long minutes passed until finally,
Exhausted, she pushed out silky twin lambs one after the other.
I let out a sigh of relief and felt an inexplicable sense
Of satisfaction in that her struggle had ended so successfully.
The ewe regained her strength and rose from the dust
To lick her two new babies lying beside her.

When the boys saw that she had finished,
They left their snacks, and wordlessly approached the ewe.
Before she could begin cleaning her twins, shockingly,
The younger boy kicked the ewe in her side,
And in her weakened state, she fell over on her unsteady legs.
Shocked at the sudden cruelty, I tried to understand,
Tried to find a reason for the willful abuse,
But there was none, they were just cruel young boys.

The older boy picked up the newborn twins by their skinny
Legs and carried them upside down towards the dusty trail.
While the lambs bleated pitifully, the boys chatted in Arabic
Seemingly oblivious to the lambs' suffering.
They stopped at the wide dirt road at the edge of the clearing
And stood there awhile as if waiting for something.
I shouted to them, telling them not to hold the lambs like that
And to give the ewe time to care for them and recover.

A. E. Hayoun

They looked at me as if they did not understand,
And I wanted to believe that maybe they didn't,
But the exhaustion of the ewe was obvious
And the cries of the lambs could not possibly be ignored.
The boys knew it was cruel, they just did not care.

The sound of a diesel engine roared in the distance
Approaching through the forest along the dirt road.
Around the bend, an old blue tractor came into sight
Driven by two boys about ten and fourteen years old,
Though the elder looked as exhausted as a forty-year-old.
I stayed to watch; I could not look away
As the boys prodded and kicked the ewe and her twins,
Loading them into a small cage precariously attached
To the back of the old tractor.

The poorly soldered cage pitched wildly under their weight.
It seemed it would break and fall off the tractor,
But the young boys climbed on top without noticing.
As the tractor drove off, the cage tilted dangerously downwards
Causing the ewe to roll on her side.
Unable to right herself, the ewe crushed
Her silky newborn twins between the bars of the cage.
The pitiful bleats and baa-s of the ewe and her twins
Fell on deaf ears as none of the boys moved to help them.

The boys on top of the cage signaled to the boy driver
That they were all aboard and the tractor left the clearing,
Leaving behind diesel fumes and an echo of faint little bleats.
The clearing was silent save for the cawing of crows
That had come to eat the abandoned afterbirth.

INSECTS

The insects in Israel are biblical.
They infest, swarm, and sting like all the rest,
But they hop through ancient battlefields,
Burrow under Judean ruins,
And stridulate from the branches of the terebinth trees.

In the land of milk and honey,
It is not the honey of the bee the Jews were promised,
But the honey of tamarim, silan from the date palms.
Their fallen fruit attracts the endless swarms of summer flies.

Scorpions, black and beige, burrow and sting in the Negev.
Loathed and feared, they are the desert mercenaries,
Rovers of dunes and mountains.

The proverbial ant of King Shlomo still lives in Israel,
Industriously building nests and storing food,
It feasts on fallen grapes and the leftover terumah.

The desert locust remains unchanged.
Descendants of those that plagued Israel and Egypt.
In the summer, they still swarm over holy land crops,
But diminished with time's steady passing is our fear
Of the arbe midbari and the famines they once caused.

How did the praying mantis receive its Hebrew name?
With its folded arms raised to his camel-like neck,
Not clasped in personal supplication,
But raised in praise like King Shlomo raised his arms
Upon the completion of the first Beit HaMikdash.
Thus, the praying mantis was given the Hebrew name
Gamal Shlomo, King Shlomo's camel.

In the Negev desert there is a hideous insect.
It is neither a scorpion nor spider but resembles both.
The harmless camel spider is feared for no reason,
Other than its horrible visage and immense size.
It is exceptionally fast but its bite is utterly harmless.

A. E. Hayoun

The white spirals in the desert are the hilazon midbari.
They hibernate in the sand most of the year,
Emerging with the rains, they survive for only a few weeks.
Just long enough to feed, mate, and lay their eggs in the sand.
They die slowly in the heat, leaving behind
Sun-bleached shells scattered endlessly across the Negev.

A sure sign of spring is the arrival of the ladybug,
The parat moshe rabeinu, the Moshe cow beetle.
Named for its cow-like spots, and inexplicably,
After our most humble prophet, Moshe Rabeinu.

In these biblical lands, time will pass, as it always does,
But the insects will continue to speak of a time before now
When they swarmed around temples and kings,
Hopped alongside our judges and priests,
And were slithering witnesses to our legends and miracles.

SHEPHERDING

With spring comes the shepherding,
The guiding of Bovidae through desert plains,
Following the growth of transient spring grasses.
The anxious moving of hundreds of hooved feet,
A race to devour as many plants as possible
Before the arrival of the scorching summer in the month of Iyar.

Shepherding is a skill and one with many methods.
Some old shepherds instruct only their loyal dogs
With small head movements and flicks of their hands,
And according to their command, the dogs herd the flocks.
They are an experienced team, working together as one.

There are shepherds who move their flocks
Using shrill whistling sounds and short cries.
Their whistle language can be heard across the desert,
But is only understood by sheepdog, shepherd, and flocks.

Some shepherds have help from their children,
Some are as young as four or five years old.
Barefoot and lively, they prod goats gone astray
And tattle to their fathers about sheep that escape the fold.

Sometimes the children are the shepherds themselves.
They drive forty head of sheep across the highways
With only a stick and their big, little voices
"burring" and prodding the sheep forward.
If a sheep dawdles as it is crossing, it receives
A firm kick with a little foot to its hindquarters.

Great black tents and rusty water trucks
Spring up in foothills around the forests and plains.
The tents house for a season a family and their herds.
The family will graze the goats and fatten them up all spring
To be ready for the early summer slaughter.

Of the shepherdess we hear too little,
But she too tends her herds in the Negev,
Or rather those of her husband.

Her portion is one of double work and double hardship.
For while she protects and provides for her herds,
She also protects and provides for her children
Who live with her in the tent and wander with her herds.

Her fat lambs and shaggy goats are sold
For as much or more than her male competitors' flocks,
But she receives no credit for her backbreaking labors,
As the flocks she tended are sold under a man's name.
As a Bedouin shepherdess, she cannot expect any more
Or work any less.

Springtime shepherding is arduous work
That finishes so abruptly at the end of spring
Following the birthing and the fattening of flocks.
When the grazing is finished, the herds are sold,
The tents are folded, and the water trucks depart
Leaving us suddenly in summer.

SPECIAL

Walking on the trail under the early summer sun,
North towards Sansana, past the blooming almond orchard
Where the scent still lingers but the pink blossoms
Have fallen out of sight beyond the ridge.

Without ever intentionally seeking, I always find
Something special in the Negev, or perhaps it finds me.
Beside the trail, a cluster of squeaky green grasses
Seem thrilled to have outgrown deep winter dirt
And finally burst forth into spring.
Their lushness (a word used sparingly in the Negev)
Draws me to sit by them on a large boulder of flint
Mottled in a rainbow of earth-tone colors.

The Negev is nearing the end of its seasonal bloom.
The dry-packed desert dirt around me is waiting
For the last touches of rain to draw out
The hidden wildflowers that wait patiently within.

Looking into the grass behind me,
There is an impression of a stone circle
Protruding in lumpy shapes beneath the grass.
Stepping from stone to stone with cautious feet,
I now stand in the stone circle at the top of the small hill,
Its center is like the crater of a small volcano long silenced.

The winds whistle overhead but a stillness
Pervades the air in the stone circle's center.
In the sea of grass, the scattered stones appear
To be the only solid objects preventing me
From sinking into the earth to be lost to time forever.

There is something special about the ruin.
The grasses beyond are nearly all burnt from the early
Summer sun, but inside the ruin the grasses flourish.
What nourishes their roots?
From whence is this powerful growth?

The amount of scattered stone suggests that it had once been

A. E. Hayoun

A rounded building with a domed beehive roof.
What could have been the purpose of a circular building
Isolated in the middle of the Negev desert?
The stones give me no clues,
And no serpent appears to answer my questions,
So, I climb out of the far side of the ruin.

As I step through deep grasses,
I nearly fall into a great yawning pit that lies open
Like a mouth in the ground before me.
Dizzy from looking into the unexpected depth of the pit,
I sit down immediately and crawl to its edge.
The two-meter-wide pit exhales cold subterranean air.
Had I missed my step, I would have fallen six meters down.

I throw a pebble inside and wait for it to reach the bottom,
When a great gust of wind and feathers belches out
Of the opening as twenty or so doves fly towards the sun.
I wait for my eyes to adjust to the darkness of the pit,
Squinting to see details of the interior,
As downy feathers rain down from the sky.

It is not a natural cave but a time-worn cistern
With plastered walls for catching rain and dew.
Cautiously circling the cistern,
I see indistinguishable figures scratched into the plaster.
Are they drawings? Or markings used to convey a message?
Their hidden purpose does not matter as much
As the fact that the drawings simply exist.
They are evidence of the people who lived here before,
The desert dwellers who drank the Negev rains,
And lived or worshipped in the stone circle's embrace.

WRITTEN

The camels live, eat, and rest in the hot dunes.
At a distance, they are a delight to my eyes.
When they are nearby, I approach them quietly,
To bask in their company and stroke their bristly sides.

Near or far, I photograph them living their lives.
When we are in the forest together,
They graze while I watch them from the shade.
When they are out in the heat of the day,
They sit on folded legs in the hot desert.

We are rarely together, me and the camels.
I live my life in my home, and they in theirs,
I never rush to them or force my company upon them.
We find one another in a natural way
And the enjoyment of our company is mutual.

My walks to the forest, no two are the same.
The magic of the desert remains unchanged.
The pottery that waits for me, the views I see
Are all spontaneously beautiful.
The caves I enter, the meadows I find,
Nothing is planned but somehow
It is all written in the sand.

A. E. Hayoun

CHASE

Wandering boldly into the Negev I love,
My feet have never hesitated
Nor has my appetite for dune or ruin,
Camel or view ever diminished.
Walking beyond the empty plain,
Where Suleiman's tent is but a seasonal memory,
I climbed ridges toward a fallow desert vineyard,
Determined to live on, tiny bright green grape leaves
And tendrils grew from the old stumps that remained.

Past the vineyard, a great distance from the forest foothills,
Far from the camels I knew, three camels were grazing.
I approached them slowly and stopped at a distance,
To enjoy their peaceful presence and slow grazing.
While I was taking their pictures, out from behind the camels
A white SUV roared over the ridge.
Spewing dust plumes and disturbing the peace of the desert
The vehicle scared the camels into a hobbled run.
And though I never had a reason to run away in the Negev,
Instinct told my legs to run away and to not stop.

My feet pounded sand and I stumbled in hidden holes
As I ran away from the well-worn dirt track.
Blind with adrenaline as the truck sped towards me,
I ran straight into a briar-filled gully
Oblivious to the thorns that tore at my pants and shirt.
Out of breath, I stood my ground in the thorny briar.
The vehicle had slowed and was driving cautiously
Off the dirt track, snapping dry thorny branches
As it approached the briar.
I stood facing the truck as it approached.
With the yishuv in the distance and the desert
Beyond the briar perfectly drivable,
There was no place to run and no purpose in a scream.
Despite the instinct to run,
There was no instinct to pull out my boot knife.
It might have only made things worse.

His truck bumper crushed the briar in front of me

The Camel in the Forest

As he could drive no deeper into it.
Through the windshield I saw an old man wearing
A red and white keffiyeh held in place with a black agal.
His age made me angrier, old enough to be a grandfather,
He was old enough to know better.
Rolling down his window, smiling with yellow teeth,
He opened his mouth to speak or laugh,
But I did not wait for him to speak the first word.
Yelling over the engine, I asked what he wanted,
But there was no explanation I would accept
For a man chasing down a woman with his truck.
He laughed hoarsely at me, wheezing for a few moments,
Until he asked me why I was near his camels.
Adrenaline had subsided mostly to anger
But now the anger began to turn into exhaustion.
I told him I was out walking and saw them
To which he pointedly asked why I ran away.
"Why did you chase me?" I replied.

I did not wait for his answer, but commanded my legs
To find the courage to walk.
I squeezed myself between the briar and his truck bumper,
And for a moment, between briar and bumper,
I was scared he would tell someone
Hiding behind the window tint to throw me into the truck.
Or that he would just run me over.
But I pushed swimming knees past the truck
And the tobacco stench that wafted out from it.
Nothing happened and I quickened my pace.

The truck stayed parked as I walked quickly in the direction
Of familiar plains and ridges towards yishuv and home.
As I was walking, I heard the truck engine idling behind me.
The further I walked the angrier I felt.
An old man thought it would be funny to intimidate me,
To chase a grown woman in his truck and trap her
In some bushes to meaninglessly interrogate her,
Laugh at her, and make her feel small.
Because how dare I walk confidently alone in the desert,
And go where I had only ever seen men go.
To enjoy the views of the desert, the wild camels,
And the freedom of nature in the Negev.

I walked up the last ridge and looked toward the yishuv
Quiet and golden in the late afternoon sun.
I stood for a while on that flat high ground
And looked back to where three camels had been.

TREASURE

I don't believe that mountains and hills
Are just empty pieces of earth rising above sea level.
Nothing more than towering piles of bedrock, dirt, and loam.
When I look at the mountains I see a story, an adventure,
The possibility of treasure hidden long ago
Waiting to be found. Or maybe a long-lost animal
Or the fossil of some unknown creature, yet to be discovered.

When I ask other people what they think,
What could be within the mountains and hills,
They either shrug or tell me it's just bedrock and soil.
They often tell me if there was something special
Hidden inside mountains, then we would see it
When new roads are built through mountain ranges.
But I think the mountains know
When people come to cut them open.

They pull back their treasures and hide their secrets
Keeping them hidden from man and his machinery.
The mountains allow the cuts and the roads to be paved,
But they heal their wounds slowly over time.
The foliage and trees grow back over the wound,
Hiding the mountains' secret nighttime growth.
When one day the mountains will knit shut their wounds
With their secrets still hidden in underground peace.

The mountains wait for the walkers and wanderers
Who adore their views and come caressing with their steps.
To the hikers, the mountains reveal their mysteries.
Their secrets of geodes and scrolls, fossils, and gemstones
Do rest and be waiting to greet the wanderer
Who is searching, not raiding.

A. E. Hayoun

WADI

Though my boot knife was always with me,
I never had cause to use it.
Until one day I used it to help an animal.

In a wadi, not far from the forest,
The rainwater that had filled it briefly in spring
Had begun to dry under the summer sun
Leaving a stinking mud in its center
And green grasses flourishing on either side.

While returning home from a walk in the forest,
I heard whinnying from the far side of the wadi.
Following the sound, I walked until I saw her,
A brown mare in apparent distress
Tethered by the side of the wadi with a long rope.

She was snorting and shaking,
Pulling against the rope which was tied to an iron spike
That had been sunk into the mud at the bottom of the wadi.
The length of the tether gave her no more than
A small semicircle of ground to pace.
And while the grasses were still flourishing around the wadi,
The grasses within her reach were trampled and dry.

She seemed to have been tethered there for a long time.
Her flanks were sweaty under early summer sun
And there was no fresh water or water trough near her.
Though she was not the first tethered horse
I had found while walking in the desert plains,
She was the first I had found left without water for so long.

I do not understand the reason for this tethering in isolated areas
But it is often done to Bedouin horses in springtime.
I sat for a while at the wadi's edge, watching her distress,
Debating whether to help her or leave her.
If I cut her tether then she could find water
Or make her way back to her owners. I hoped.

I climbed down into the wadi into the soft sludge at its center,

The Camel in the Forest

Took out my small knife, and I began to saw at the rope.
Progress was slow as the rope was thick and gummy,
But twists of rope started to unfurl as I made progress.
All the while I kept an eye on the mare pacing above.

When the rope was halfway cut, I heard the sound
Of tires bouncing on the dirt track above.
I left the rope and crawled to hide behind a large karkash.
Though my intentions were good,
I wasn't sure everyone would see them that way.

As the truck parked and voices in Arabic came closer,
I climbed quietly up the wadi hidden behind bushes.
Reaching the forest, concealed from view,
I watched two Bedouin men load the mare into their trailer.

Dust plumes swirled around the trailer as the truck
Bounced on the dirt track in the direction it had come.
The rope lay still at the edge of the wadi,
And the semicircle of trampled ground was empty and quiet.
From under a shaded tree, near the entrance to a small cave,
I sat for a while and watched the sun begin to set.

A. E. Hayoun

HIRAN

Har Hiran stands proudly in the northern Negev.
A mountain plateau with all the Negev in view.
To the north proud Lahish and to the south deep Arava.

At its summit, the rocks are strange, quite different
From the rocks found at its base.
These rocks, not easily disturbed on the mountaintop,
Out of sight and nearly forgotten, tells the mountain's story.

Under blinding sunlight and jealous piercing winds,
Great slices of red and brown rocks lay scattered,
Polished smooth by the endless flying sands.

At the center of the plateau are four cornerstones,
The remains of an ancient building.
Once a house or temple built solely of speckled dolomite
And red and brown chert, the walls now lay fallen
Piled up in great heaps on the mountain plateau.

I enter the building, not over the fallen walls,
But under the invisible lintel under which I turn
And look out of the building from its entrance
At its view into the Negev.

The view chosen by the people who lived here before,
The guardians of the Negev, the people of Hiran.

BIRTH

Walking on the trail one day,
I came upon a scene of great consequence.
A story of birth, love, courage, and desire,
That unfolded before my eyes.

At the edge of the trail ahead of me,
I saw a smudge of reddish orange concealed in the bushes.
Tall fuzzy ears of a rare Negev fox
Quivered above its hiding place.
The fox was not hiding from me,
But looking intently beyond the trail,
Into the valley of terebinths and carob trees below.

I stopped in the shade and watched the fox,
Using my binoculars to follow his gaze.
From pine-bough shade across the trail,
I heard before I saw the object of his attention,
Cries of pain and distress were audible to the entire forest.

Out of reach of the burning summer sun,
A cream-colored she-goat was ambling
In circles around a pine tree.
Her legs staggered and shook as her bleating cries increased.

Through my binoculars, I saw between her hind legs,
Her breached baby goat stuck half in and half out.
She knew all was not well
And her ringing cries told the forest so.

I moved cautiously closer useless to her painful distress,
But I watched her intensely hoping for the best.
I was not the only one watching and waiting,
The Negev fox was unmoved watching her just as intensely.
A fox in the afternoon sun is either sick or wholly desperate,
And at a distance, this fox appeared to be both.

The she-goat's cries turned to bleating grunts
And within a few minutes, miraculously,
Her newborn fell to the ground in the dry grass at her hooves.

To her relief and my own, her kid started bleating
And walking shakily in the grass.

The she-goat returned to her resting and grazing,
But it was the fox who sprang into action.
Sunk low to the ground on swift little paws,
The fox rushed across the trail
And down the side of the valley
Towards the mother goat and her kid.

Whether the fox was running for the afterbirth in the grass
Or the young, tender baby goat,
The fox never made it to its desired prize.
Through my binoculars, the she-goat's rectangular pupils
Showed no fear nor hesitation, just a steady gaze
Trained on the fleet lanky fox running towards her.

With two hooves pushed into the ground,
Her hard head butted into the oncoming fox's red snout
And sent the fox sprawling down the steep valley decline.

The gentle she-goat had vanquished the rabid fox,
Who did not ascend from the valley to try the she-goat again.
The fox disappeared into the forest below,
His reddish coat concealing his carnivorous shame
At being bested by an herbivore on such a fine summer's day.

Dust

I walk from forest to forest,
Into deserts of Yehuda and Arava,
Between the resting places
Of the illustrious matriarchs and pitied Idit,
Through the Gateway of the Negev.

The Negev seems empty in the afternoon quiet.
The desert residents take shelter at midday,
They hide in burrow, den, and home.
All is still except for the slow-blinking eyes
Of the lizard, crow, and sun.

But at midday in the forest,
I sit in the sun at the entrance to the anthill,
Where the ants' ordered industriousness
Is unbothered by my gaze.

Staring into the shimmering heat,
I watch fields of green and gold waver in the hot wind.
The wind sings through the tree branches above me,
Combing my hair, encircling my neck.

Parts of me are swept up in its current
And float into the desert, where I happily become
Dust of the earth and sand in the wind.

A. E. Hayoun

IRIS

The Negev iris in the Arad fortress,
Beautiful bloom of the desert.
Brown like the sand she grows defiantly from
Not purple like the iris that grows in milder climes
Where color is not an extravagance.

Brown beauty, made more beautiful
Because she blooms where others wilt.
Flower queen of the arid, flourishing in the desert,
Protected like a queen in her ancient fortress.

Negev iris, I admire her.
Her natural beauty blooms only after
Seasons of rooting and waiting.

She does not rush the natural process
Of finding her place, laying down roots,
And building herself up under the sun.
She drinks the rains and tends to her needs,
Allowing the sun to darken her hidden petals.

Then one day she is ready,
And the Negev need wait no longer,
For her bloom to captivate and enthrall
Until the day arrives for her to wilt.

RUIN

Along a dusty trail, I walked southward
Towards a valley I had never explored.
The area was different than others I knew,
Notably in the lack of animals,
Both their prints and their presence.

Standing at the top of a hot desert ridge,
Before I descended into the valley,
I was shocked at the view that stretched out before me.
Angry heat flushed my face
And I felt a cold shudder on my skin.

The valley below was a wasteland of trash and garbage.
Once a wild desert valley, home to desert fauna,
The valley before me was a ruin
Of grey concrete and primary-colored waste.

Discarded toilets, broken drywall, and building materials
Stretched the length of the valley.
Broken glass of doors and windows
Were shattered over ancient limestone.

Years of construction debris was strewn everywhere
Mixed with heaps of residential trash and plastic.
The seeping filth soaked deep into the holy land,
The stench of fetid refuse hung in the hot air.

I descended the valley and walked through the mess,
Closing my nose to the stink,
Grateful for the thick soles of my boots.
Oils of every color and purpose mixed on the ground
With discarded batteries creating a corrosive glue
That choked the sand and soil.
The only plant that attempted to grow in that valley
Was the resilient saltbush, but smothered in filth
Even its growth was stunted.

This dumping ground was no accident,
Nor was it long forgotten.

There were new tire marks next to stinking bags of trash,
Old waste and new moldered side by side.
They came to dump their refuse and debris,
Knowing they would not be caught.

Whoever they were, they cared more about
Avoiding a fee at the landfill than the fact
That their waste was seeping into groundwater,
Poisoning our land, and ruining our birthright.

DUNE

Walking home with a heavy heart,
Hands empty but crossed arms full of indignation,
Piercing anger, and helpless desire.

They ruin my forest and mar my desert,
They wrong this land.
But what help do I have to offer?
How can I right the wrongs?

Blaming, raging, scratching, and gnashing,
I stamped over dusty ridge and ranted through desert gully.
Wishing I could find the criminal for the crime.

Purple dusk in the gully and orange evening sun overhead.
Suddenly, little rocks came sliding down from the ridge above
And scattered near my feet at the bottom of the gully.

I saw the hooves before I saw the rider,
Stamping dust into columns in the air.
My eyes followed the hooves upwards
To fetlocks, haunches, and saddle.
A great red saddle covered in colorful embroidery
And multi-layered tassels was strapped
Around the broad back of a rawboned stallion.

As the horse whinnied and paced along the top of the ridge,
A Bedouin rider bedecked in black robes and a large turban
Sat rigidly against the jerky movements of his anxious steed.
He stared down at me visibly fuming in the gully below,
Teeth grinding grains of sand, I stared back.

Gold hour sun glowed hazel in his eyes framed by keffiyeh
And dark eyebrows that furrowed down at me,
As my own furrowed back at him.
For a few moments, time stopped
Only the sand skipped over the ground,
Then I nodded and he nodded,
The horse nickered, and the desert winds
Blew to the east, carrying us to our homes in the Negev.

A. E. Hayoun

EUCALYPTUS

A fragrant snapping of dry green crescents
Under red-bark branches, past smooth twisted trunks,
Beneath a eucalyptus canopy under which I wander.

I breathe deeply cineole and camphor,
And gather fallen branches to fragrance my home.
The eucalyptus roots twist deeply.

Digging through loam, sand, and rock,
Pushing downwards through the waters,
The sea, bohu v'tohu, beyond the abyss,
Downwards from the ceiling of Tebel
To nourish their fragrant canopy
And draw upwards the color of magma.

Blossoms are held in brown pedicles like earthen chalices.
Petals and stamen like frothy orange wine waver
In temperate breeze beneath the shade of their mother tree.

The blossoms like grown daughters ready themselves
To leave home forever at summer's end.
Departing, they leave their fallen calyptrae
Like forsaken crowns that roll in the wind
On the ground at my resting feet.

GMALIM

Autumn fog engulfs the forest, birdsong rises from the mists.
I am awake before dawn and set out into the fog
Towards the forest to photograph its autumnal likeness.
The forest is wrapped in a misty morning blanket of fog,
The fog changes from grey to blue to gold
As it is scattered by the sunrise.

Sitting on a sela, I watch the forest remove veil after veil
Of fog and mist as it is touched by morning light.
From within the fog there is a muffled sound,
A slow movement of heavy feet approaching where I sit.

Where golden dew dances airborne among the branches,
Large tan heads emerge, floating for a moment ahead
Of their bodies before the rest of the camel
Strides out from the fog.
The camels have awakened from their forest slumber.

Just a few at first, then five, ten, and more.
Walking out of the fog towards where I sit,
Some thirty camels ploddingly step over sand and stone.
As they approach my boulder, they pass me on both sides,
Like waves breaking against an island.

As if in a dream, I open my arms and stretch myself
To reach their wiry coats as they brush past my fingers.
The fog has cleared and the sun has risen,
Behind me the camels begin their morning grazing.

Mothers with still-swollen udders walk slowly
With their calves by their side.
The large males smell of urine and musk,
And though they seem anxious, they are all docile,
Passing me by as if I have become part of the boulder.

I notice the camels are all cruelly hobbled.
Only the nursing calves walk freely next to their mothers.
Cruel ropes tie the camels skinny front ankles together,
Fifty centimeters of rope perpetually taunt, less than half

A. E. Hayoun

The length of the camels' natural stride of one meter.

The males seem the most constrained by their ropes,
Each step reverberates up their legs
As their stride comes up too short.
Sadly, the females and the elderly are more resigned.
Each step the older camels take is shaky, almost jaunty,
Learned from years of walking with a broken stride.

The older camels have calloused flesh that grows like a ridge
Over the rope that cuts deeply into their ankles.
What seemed like a slow peaceful stride out of the forest
Were cautious steps of hobbled gentle giants,
Stepping carefully so as not to fall or trip.
With one misstep they would fall uncontrollably
In a fatal tangle of rope, neck, and legs.

The elderly, bony and slow, take much longer to graze.
While I sat observing them, I calculated the time
They would need to find and eat their fill before sunset
Demanded their nightly return to the forest.

Watching them reminded me of many years ago
When I rode a camel at a renaissance fair in America.
I climbed a small ladder to a high platform and at the top
Only a hairy tan hump saddled in red and tassels was visible.
For all I knew it could have been a mechanical camel
Because I never saw its face or the rest of it
Over the elaborate rigging it wore.

Urged forward by a ridiculously dressed fool,
The camel took a few plodding steps around a dirt track
In a closed dirt yard, well-worn from endless pacing.
I will never forget that ride and the jerky stride
Of the hobbled camel, each step cut short
And reverberated up through the camel's joints.

I cannot imagine that a camel in captivity can live
To its natural, almost human, life expectancy of forty years.
They would die sooner, if not from disease or malnutrition,
Then surely from insanity.
Because instinctually they must know where they belong.

The Camel in the Forest

Roaming great expanses of wild earth in herds
Where they can run together and mate and feed.

I left my boulder to walk among the camels.
My presence did not disturb them, but they watched me
From under long lashes as I watched their young calves
Frolic and nurse while their mothers grazed
On dry grasses soon to be lost to muddy winter.
The sun rose higher in the sky, casting longer shadows
Of those otherworldly creatures, the camels from the forest.

A. E. Hayoun

REPORT

From among the wandering Jews led by Moshe,
Twelve of them were chosen by HaShem's command
To scout and assess the land that would be their inheritance.
Twelve men of worth, one from each tribe,
Were sent to judge the Negev and assess its terrain.

From Tzin to Hevron, the twelve began their journey,
Walking up through the land where my house now stands.
In Hevron, some of the people were as large as fearful giants,
Descendants of the Nephelim, of men and fallen angels.

In the wadi Eshkol, they found grape clusters
Large enough that two men were needed to carry them.
There were figs and pomegranates aplenty.
From there, they returned south towards the desert of Paran.

There they recounted to Moshe and the Jews
What they had learned of the promised land.
Was it good or bad? Were the people strong or weak?
And of their cities, were they fortified or exposed?

The scouts told of the land, prosperous and fertile,
A land of many fruits and the promised milk and honey.
But they reported their fears of the giants
And shared their doubts about overtaking the walled cities.

Eleven scouts sowed their doubt among the Jews,
The same Jews who by HaShem's miracles
Had been nourished in the desert,
The Jews who had no reason to doubt the word of HaShem.

Only one scout, Calev, spoke up for HaShem's promise,
And of His assurance of victory against the giants.
For their doubt, the eleven scouts and the Jews in the desert
Were punished, they and their descendants.
They would never enter the land that was their inheritance.

Only the children of Calev returned to the land and shared
The covenant made between Avraham and HaShem.

The Camel in the Forest

And here we remain, living in our promised land
Because of Calev's belief in HaShem's covenant
And in this land given to our forefathers.

I now sit on the banks of nahal Bsor,
In the land of Eshkol where the grapes still grow.
The air becomes chilled as the sun sets,
And I return to my home near Yatir,
East of Eshkol, between Tzin and Hevron.

A. E. Hayoun

DESERTESS

Walking in the forest, sometimes I remember
That the world is unkind and not always safe.
Someone leaves the trash behind, the camels have owners,
Strangers make the tire tracks; there are others in the forest.

It feels like the forest is mine; the birds, and the camels
Feel like they belong to me, just as I belong to the desert.
These natural gifts fill my heart with joy
And draw me out into the desert, day after day.

I feel secure in this love, but often the shiver knows better.
When my skin prickles, foretelling an unknown danger,
I get off the dirt track and hide myself from view.

From my hiding place, at the mouth of a cave,
Or behind conjoined pines with my eyes closed,
I hear distant voices in Arabic draw closer and pass me by.

They will never see the woman alone in the forest
The same way I feel being the woman alone in the forest.
I wish the forest were denser, fuller.
More trees, more animals, more people, more women.

Where are the women who walk in the forest?
Surely there are more than just me.
The women who enter caves, pace the fields,
And walk the forest knowing they belong.

Even if my voice quavers or my knees knock together,
I know I belong here, here where the forest knows me.
My love never falters, it only grows deeper,
Knowing my love is rare and its expression unique.

So ever onwards, forever forward,
Into forest and desert, valley, and cave,
Ever deeper into the Negev, my home.

HORVAT YATIR

Ancient ruins facing Eshtamoa,
Lay beautifully exposed in unprotected decay.
Boundless ruins stretch over a great tract of land,
Over one thousand dunam of hills and valleys,
Once a thriving Levite city in the region of Yatir.

I collect pieces of shattered pottery, parts of the Levite story,
And wonder how they lived and how their city fell into ruin.
The remains of countless arched ceilings, stone pillars,
And stone lintels at the entrance to caves cover the land.

On a hilltop plateau are large gouges in the earth,
Forced upheaval of stones between an ancient oil press
And the toppled stone walls of once a great building.
Thieves had come and stolen pieces of history,
Pieces of Horvat Yatir meant for us all.

History meant to be preserved in perpetuity,
For all of us to learn how our people once lived
In their stone homes and caves in the heart of Yatir.
The artifacts that we can only imagine are now gone.
Lost to a dark world of vanished glory,
More lost than when they were buried.

I stand inside the once-silent grave, now an empty pit,
I hold some bones fragments and a neck of a jug,
Recovered remains, history left behind.
Had Horvat Yatir been protected and preserved
There would be so much more of it left to enjoy,
But in the Negev, the ruins are left as they are,
Exposed to the elements, victim to greedy looting.

A. E. Hayoun

GIVING

In the northern-most desert,
Where the Negev becomes Yehuda v'Shomron,
Ancient Susya rests silently in the sun,
Keeping her secrets, and welcoming new visitors.
To the North is the cave purchased by Avraham
In which to bury his beloved Sara, The Cave of the Patriarchs.
Forever a site of comfort and return for the Jews.
These ancient sites lie over a line they call "green,"
A border between Israel and her ancestral lands.
A border that must be crossed to visit our heritage sites.

Over the border, on the way to these sites,
All along the highway are large red signs.
Written in English, Hebrew, and Arabic,
The signs warn of imminent death to any Jew
Who passes the sign and enters the Arab town beyond.
It is not one town with one sign, it is many towns
In great swathes throughout our ancestral lands.
Jews drive past these signs every day.
People calling for our deaths is our everyday.

There have been accidents, Jews who have entered
An Arab town by mistake, and unless the Israeli military
Can arrive in time, the Jews will be beaten and lynched.
Their blood used to spell out the enemies' hate.
There have been times, that an Arab has come forward
And has stood between the Jew and the lynch mob.
All of this has happened, more than once,
Not in some distant land or written in a foreign newspaper,
But just a drive north from my house.

But it does not deter us, we drive onwards to Susya
To read the ancient story of Creation
And the first mention of our holy Shabbat
Written out in ancient mosaic.
We visit our ancestors in the Cave of the Patriarchs,
Even if we can only ten days out of the year.

And why is that, why is time limited for the Jews at our cave?

The Camel in the Forest

It is no longer an ancient colonizing enemy denying us entry,
But it was Moshe Dayan who first gave up control and access
To our ancestors in Hevron,
In hopes that it would prevent another Hevron Massacre.

Similar decisions have since been made with the same logic:
If the Jews give up something that is theirs by every right,
Maybe the enemy that hates us will make peace with us.
This flawed thinking has led to failure every single time.
Putting our ancestral lands under our enemies' control,
The enemy who regularly destroys our heritage sites.

When Gush Katif was given unconditionally in 2005
To the Palestinians by Prime Minister Sharon,
The Jews ethnically cleansed themselves from the Gaza Strip.
Synagogues were destroyed by Jews, dead Jews exhumed,
And the Jews living in Gush Katif were removed
From their homes, not by the enemy, but by fellow Jews.
Now it is gone, nothing remains of the Gush Katif paradise
That once was, and what has replaced it is a small land
Of great corruption, endlessly a hotbed of hatred for the Jews.

Will we ever learn or will we always forget?
A hungry beast is never satisfied, no matter how much
They are fed, they consume it all until they are sick,
And then return to demand more.

A. E. Hayoun

Pillar

Standing in the desert,
Peeling my skin under the sun.
Planting mandrakes in the sand,
Brushing knots from my stomach.

There is a vibration in the desert,
A humming through the wind.
There is a standing in my soul,
A feeling before knowing.

The Earth tremors and thrums,
My breath catches in my throat.
Then my eyes see the pillar of sand by day,
Moving like a thousand fox feet so swiftly
It does not touch the ground.

Birds wheel overhead
And are pulled into the orbit of the powerful vortex.
A great beast of sand and wind,
A golem of air rages in the desert on a heedless trajectory.

It engulfs desert draff,
The lightest travels up into the vortex
To be spat out again over the Negev,
And the heaviest: rocks, tents, camels, and trees
Are shaken in its path and returned to stillness.

I do not turn away but only close my eyes
As electric wind spins me around
To face the Negev in the Land.

A pillar of sand in sunlight,
Vibrating from heaven to earth.
A vortex from above wakes my spirit from slumber,
And opens my mouth in praise.

TZAVOA

Darkness threatens the human mammal with all the unseen
But it is the early dawn when the beasts
Leave the shadows to return to their dens.
And if the carnivore found no feast that night,
And the sunrise heralds the hour to return to diurnal den,
The beasts may choose not to suffer
Another day of sleepless hunger.
They will be desperate in their final search
To find or make a toothsome kill.

Waking early, I set out toward the forest
With the dog for company to watch the sunrise.
At this convergence of night and morning,
Moonglow and sunrise, birds awaken in chorus.
The predators hurry across dew-wet streets
Towards forest and shadowed hills.
At my side, the dog trots briskly, alert to all the sounds.
The moon shifts to the west and south,
Faint light in the east grows slowly stronger highlighting
Familiar figures of early risers wrapped in tlitot,
Walking towards synagogue for gratitude and prayer.
Making my own thanks for the purple clouds
That skip across a golden sky, I turn from the side street
Toward the last kikar before the forest.

Under the sculpture of peace at the center of the kikar
Are three hunched figures standing in the shadow.
I squint in the still-dark morning and blink twice more
Then I see more clearly their striped bodies,
Salivating jaws opening and closing soundlessly,
Sloped haunches, and too-small eyes staring.
The breeze carries with it a light stench
Of stinging musk and rotten meat.
At my side, the dog breathes soundlessly,
But I see the change in his stance, his fur standing on end,
And his hackles raised baring his canine teeth.
A scent of metallic blood from their rancid breath
Wafts over to us on the wind.
The hyenas' wild smiles and fearless stances

Block our way forward, and the shiver up my spine
Tells me not to run away.

Driven up from deep Arava to the streets of my yishuv,
Ravenous hyenas are not intimidated by large prey,
Their relatives just south and west of us in Africa
Are devouring prey much larger and more formidable
Than yishuv woman and domesticated dog.
Armed with sharp teeth and most likely rabies,
The hyenas have the advantage and the two of us outnumbered.
But I see that they are uneasy,
Shifting paw to paw, feeling out of their element.
Six golden eyes stare, their jaws open and close
As if speaking silently or imagining their next meal.

Unhelpfully my mind recalls that the closest relation
To a hyena is the mongoose, not the wolf or the tiger,
Just the adorable meerkat and the swift mongoose.
But the slavering beasts in the path before me
Share no resemblance to anything small or adorable,
They are full-blooded carnivores, hungry at dawn.

Minutes pass and none of us have moved,
But the smallest hyena seems anxious for action.
Just as he begins to step in front of the two larger hyenas,
In a great rush of feathers, a flock of just-risen pigeons
Flies out from behind the sculpture, above the kikar,
Stirring the air around us.
The hyenas flinched, I jumped, the dog remembers to bark
And then the feeling is mutual.
The sun is rising and its best we part ways.

They pass in front of us, heads immobile,
The largest hyena makes a low cackling sound.
I heard it as a complaint for the meal they missed
And another day of hunger-filled sleep.
I begin to think that only bright daytime
Would be safest for wandering omnivores
And their canine companions.

HORVAT ANIM

Driving along the winding road through the Yatir forest,
Towards the ruins of Horvat Anim.
In a clearing dominated by great sprawling ruins,
Two carved columns stand taller than the rest.
They support the lintel of the ancient Anim synagogue.

The lintel carved with a motif of curves and vines
Is rubbed smooth and faded by time.
Inside the roofless beit knesset,
Spanning the length of the furthest wall
Is a stone bench where the Jews of old gathered
And sat for prayers and the weekly Torah reading.

Among the ruins, near the synagogue,
Is a great raised platform of stone and mortar
Whose ancient purpose remains a mystery.
Was it an altar or bima, foundation or courtyard?

Following grassy knolls and their snake-y paths
From one concealed cave to another,
I imagine the lives of each family that once lived in Anim.
The caves are countless, some with two entrances,
While some entrances are hidden,
But each cave is different in shape and surprising in size.

In the largest that opens like a great underground foyer,
There is an olive press at its center with the granite millstone
And extraction trough still in their ancient places.
Worn into the limestone floor is a groove
Where a four-legged beast of burden walked in circles
And expressed the golden oil from the olives.

In the half shade of the nearby vineyard,
We spread out a picnic of fruits and cheese,
White wine and bread to bless.

Between cave and vines, in damp autumnal grass,
Among old Anim ruins in the new Yatir forest,

We ate at our leisure, joined by the memory
Of the Jews who once prayed at Anim.

SAKIN

I am with my camels in the forest above the yishuv,
Enjoying their amusing company,
And observing these curious companions.
I enjoy a simple picnic of fruit and cheese
While I watch them go about their day.

The camels spend most of their time grazing and staring,
Fuzzy lashes half-closed, hiding large watching eyes.
Apart from the group is an old male camel
With patchy fur and a wrinkled face.
He isn't bothered by my approach, so I sit for a while
To study him and watch his behavior.

He has soft spiky fur (where it still grows)
And beautiful round feet made for walking
On hot sand and shifting rocky terrain.
With jerky steps, he grazes along the foothills.

Watching his hobbled legs stagger along the hillside,
I felt suddenly that I couldn't see his legs hobbled any longer.
I took out my boot knife and approached him slowly.
Busy grazing, and possibly too old to see me clearly,
The old camel didn't seem to care.

Kneeling beneath his barrel-like body,
His front legs and back legs on either side of me,
I paused to feel the air for any signs of fear or distress,
But there was only the camel's loud regular breathing
And steading munching from his closed mouth.

I began to saw at the thick smelly rope between his front legs.
Taunt and old, the rope gave away to my knife cord by cord.
I grasped the rope firmly for fear of chaffing the camel's legs
But his ankles were so calloused, he didn't notice at all.

The rope split and two limp ends hung from his skinny ankles.
I backed away from him, watching for a reaction,
But he only kept on chewing and gazing at nothing.
I sat back in the sand and waited for his first steps.

When he finally moved from one saltbush to the next,
Taking steps toward freedom, I watched with anticipation.
But his steps staggered the same as they had before,
And his stride was the same width
The rope had trained him to take.

Years of conditioning had shortened his stride.
Liberated from his shackles, a camel free to run,
He was still fettered by muscle memory
And imprisoned by his mind.
The old camel hobbled step by step
Down the foothills until he was out of sight.

I never saw him again,
Not out grazing nor among his tribe.
Perhaps he did finally run away,
Even if only in his mind.

MUSHROOMS

Under the streaming first rains,
Head bent to the ground; I prise out pottery
With muddy fingers, numb from the cold and wind.
Gathering pottery shards with such fervor,
As though it were firewood in the winter
Or sustenance for my children.

Newly revealed by the seasonal rains,
Not a single piece of pottery is overlooked by my hands,
But gathered in from the cold and placed in my canvas sack.
They keep me as much as I keep them.
In days of confinement, the search fuels me like a furnace
Bringing me out under the sky, in any weather.

To my surprise, in the corner of my eye,
At the edge of the yishuv, another person is out in the rain.
The man is armed with two dogs, both large and brown,
Who frisk with delight in the rain and chill.

Through the rain and mist, the dogs catch sight of me
Digging in the foothills, up near the forest.
They pull at their leads and their human follows their urging
Up to the forest over muddy desert terrain.

On the trail next to me, the man notices that I am digging.
His dogs jump excitedly at me,
Splashing in the same mud that I am kneeling in.
Shouting through the rain, and over the baying of his hounds,
The man asks me,
"GOOD MUSHROOMS THIS TIME OF YEAR?"

AGES

In the new forest,
Thinking of the ancient trees.
Where have they gone?
Givers of shelter,
Witnesses to miracles,
Shade of our ancestors.

Perhaps they went with the bears and the lions.
Carried off, never to return.
Taken for Ottoman railroad ties,
Used for rugs and meat.
But I see you
In the shimmering heat.

Ancient palms and mighty oaks,
Lions in Judah and golden bears.
A mirage,
As they will see me
Sitting in Yatir,
Ages hence.

EYES

If I squint,
The colors of the Negev blur into an ethereal sunset.

If I open my eyes slightly,
I see the Negev perhaps as it once was,
Stone houses blending with sand and sun.

If I open my eyes wider,
I see the scattered gardens,
Camels grazing, and the duhifat sunbathing

With eyes wide open,
I see it all.
The ancient, the modern; the better, the worse.

With my eyes turned inwards,
I see the Negev renewed, cared for, and cherished;
All that I long for.

With the eyes of my heart,
I see the native species returned,
Peace pervading, and the Negev as it was.

Through the eyes of my hands,
I see the work to be done, all that must be restored,
The ravaged lands to be renewed.

With the eyes of my feet,
I know the land upon which I stand.
Ancient and powerful, beautiful and precious.

With the eyes of my soul,
I see the return of the Jews.

A. E. Hayoun

BERESHIT SHELI

In the beginning, when I created for myself a new life. The new life was like a dream hovering over the surface of reality and there was great doubt under the surface of the dream. But I said, "Let there be new life!" and there was a new life. I saw that the new life was good and I separated between the dream and reality, I called the dream fulfilled and the reality made new. And I said, "Let there be great joy in this dream fulfilled and abundant courage for the new reality." And it was so. I began to live in great joy and used my new courage to face all the newness that surrounded me. And I called the new life wonderful.

It was evening and it was morning, three months.

And I said, "Let there be joy and purpose in this new life." And there was plenty. Babies were born, daily work was done, and my days were full. But there was a call on the wind and a message in the sand, that beckoned me out beyond the yishuv, into the hazy horizon towards the quiet pine forest. And I said, "Let us go beyond and discover what lies there, discover the Negev and know its lands, as I knew the lands of my childhood." I walked past the boundary of the yishuv, into stark sunlight and burning sands. I wandered into the desert and walked between endless trees.

It was evening and it was morning, six months.

And I said, "Show me your special places, your hidden delights; let me meet your swarms of fowl, the legendary camel, and the creatures that I do not know." And the sky filled with wings of every size and color, gliding on the wind, flapping through dry heat; each type of Negev native one after the other. Then the mammals and the reptiles slinked past me, acknowledged the newness of my presence, and hurried onwards to their dens and burrows. The more I wandered the more caves I found, hidden from those who do not enter the forest. Deep wadis and shaded groves, mounds of flint and sunken pits of time-lost pottery; the Negev showed it all to me.

The Camel in the Forest

It was evening and it was morning, nine months.

And I said, "This is not the Negev I imagined, not the camels in the forest, nor the wild cats; I had never seen owls in the desert or heard of special Negev snails. Nor was I expecting the ruin and waste that threatens the land; of those who do not value it and abuse it for their own sake, I knew nothing of them. And I wondered if I was alone in this knowledge of the magic and complexities of this great desert in Israel.

It was evening, and it was morning, one year.

And I said, "I love you, Negev, and I never wish to be parted from you. Neither the waste you contain nor those who threaten you will deter my love. I wish to keep you as best I can, stay with you, and learn your ways." Day after day, woman alone, I walked the Negev, watched, and learned. I hoped to find more women in the Negev, emboldened by their love of the land. Growing more trustful with each step in the Negev. Women knowing our land, reclaiming it with our feet, and in turn, reclaiming our own wilderness and deserts.

It was evening and it was morning and I stopped counting.

A. E. Hayoun

RUMBLINGS

Standing in the desert, facing the forest.
Behind me Hiran, before me, a vision as clear as the sky.

They came one by one
From burrow and den, nest and cave.
Camel and mole, orvani and jackal.
Even the tinshemet abandoned her sleep
To shimmer before me in the blazing desert sun.

The ibex from the south, the hidden caracal,
An ostrich, and the hedgehog stood before me.
The hyena I feared, an ayala from the Arava,
A bat and the hyrax, and a serious desert hare were present.

The fearful horned viper slithered to my feet.
The iridescent tzufit flitted before my eyes.
Even those lost to time joined the animals all.
The Syrian bear and wild leopard sat on furry haunches.

I waited, watching the assembly
Of all Negev creatures, beasts of land and sky.
And when they had gathered,
A shaking in the Negev reverberated up my feet
But none of the animals fled.

Sands shifted, the sun blinked,
But the assembly remained gathered before me.
A violent shaking rumbled deep in the Earth
Shattering winds and scattering sands.

The winds quieted; the sun blazed again,
And all had returned to a peaceful stillness.
But the sands had already shifted.
Something had changed
And the Negev would never be the same.
Animal and insect, reptile and bird
Looked pointedly at me and I heard their voices saying,

The Camel in the Forest

There are rumblings from Yerushalayim in Heled

First the tinshemet spread her wings and took flight.
The caracal left on padded foot.
The small tzufit disappeared into the sun.
They slithered and flew, crawled and stalked,
They left me unhurriedly to stand alone in the desert.

WAR

Nothing old. Nothing new. Everything changed. All of it true.

A. E. Hayoun

PICTURES

10.5.21

When I returned from the desert in the late afternoon,
I did not know I had been out wandering
Between the last war and the next.
I did not know that tomorrow would bring war into today.

The day had been pleasant, pleasantly regular.
I made our evening meal and we ate as a family.
But by nighttime everything had changed.

Missiles rained down on Israel from Gaza.
Like a bleeding wound the volleys of missiles
Spread from Tel Aviv to Jerusalem,
Ashkelon, and through the shfela,
They spread south towards Be'er Sheva.

The big picture: Israel at war against terrorism, again.
Muslim extremists united into terror groups,
Robing themselves in the guise of freedom fighters,
And launching barrage after barrage of missiles at Israel.

The reason for this ongoing conflict remains the same:
Radical Muslims want Israel for themselves
And mistakenly believe Jerusalem belongs only to Islam.
To fulfill these two false ideals, they attack Israel,
Aiming to kill as many Jews and Israelis as possible.

The missiles they launch rain down on our civilians,
But many fall back onto the civilians in Gaza.
Terrorism does not discriminate; everyone is an obstacle
To the ultimate goal of their absolute control of Israel.

Israel's international "allies" believe that this conflict
Has only to do with land claims in Israel,
They do not see that in the trajectory of radical Islam,
After Israel, the West is next.
The real goal is not establishing Palestine in Israel,

The Camel in the Forest

But the eradication of Western values in the Middle East
And the whole world over.

These "allies" pressure Israel to relinquish more of herself.
To carve out more of our land, give up more of our resources
In hopes of satiating the insatiable beast.
But if their citizens and country were similarly attacked,
These "allies" would immediately return fire
And without a second thought enter a full-scale war.

But the world does not allow Israel the right to self-defense
Or the right to self-determination in our indigenous land.
Days passed and more missiles fell on Israel.
The Iron Dome intercepted most,
But many struck homes and killed loved ones,
Forever marring families.

As we fled the kitchen table for the bomb shelter below,
Our prayers for safety included Israel and all her soldiers,
And the questions foremost in our minds were
"When will it end?" and "When will we be left in peace?"

Waiting in the cool bomb shelter below the house,
I thought of the small picture:
My camels in the forest, where do they take shelter?
May flowers are in bloom, and I will miss their moment.
What becomes of the flocks and herds during wartime,
What about the lambs and kids?
If I am not among them, do they remain?

A. E. Hayoun

Secure

11.5.2021

On Rosh Chodesh Sivan I did not go to the forest.
I stayed in my garden, stayed close to shelter,
Played with my babies, and kept them safe.
Overnight, wartime priorities had changed our lives,
And in the midst of uncertainty, I sought security.

Aware of all that had become
Of those rumblings in Yerushalayim in Heled,
I understood what had begun and what had changed.
But the war hadn't really begun for us
Until it began over our home
And our garden where our babies play in the sun.
The war begins when the bomb shelter at home is emptied
And its contents are replaced with our bodies seeking refuge.

White streamers trail behind racing missiles
That arch through the sky overhead,
And after the explosion of a fall or an interception,
The white rainbows that remain behind
Appear like crossed lines on the open palm of the sky.
Who can read them? Who can understand their meaning?

A single ghostly note of the sirens' song wailed
From the local schoolyard, now closed to its students.
The sirens sound and all who hear them run and weep;
Silently, tearlessly.
Parents wear masks of calm and they comfort
Their frightened children with conjured confidence,
But when they are alone, tears stream from the mask
And their voices quaver with sadness and rage,
Their clenched, worried hearts are soul-weary
Of young death and decades of hatred endured.

We become the same, all of us, just parents in Israel.
No longer separated by politics or religious observance.
Our prayers soar upward to the heavens, and we wonder,
Will they be pierced by missiles in their ascent?

MATTER

12.5.21

I did not realize how much the mind learns
Even when it does not always understand,
And how much more the ears hear when the mouth is silent.

As the reality around me began to intensify,
My Hebrew began to improve.
Instead of just sitting next to people watching the news,
I began to understand the news we were watching.

I began to understand more with each passing day of war,
And the more I understood of the life around me,
The more I began to change.
I began to understand the difference between the stories:
The ones they tell about us and the ones we tell each other.

And then they not only mattered,
But I became responsible for them.
For the history, the stories, the truths, and the lies.
I understood the responsibility of living in Israel,
Of being Israeli, of living as a Jew in our homeland.

I felt the burden of explaining our existence
And relaying the truth of life in Israel to the world.
With every debate, my confidence grew,
And my understanding deepened with each question I asked.

I began to take part, in my own small way,
In the verbal defense of my country and my home.
The lies told about Israel were lies told about me,
The wrong done to my people was wrong done to me.
I began to take it personally and let it all matter.

And when it all matters, a decision must be made,
To speak out or remain silent,
To make a difference or do nothing.
Here and now, there is no going back to oblivion.

A. E. Hayoun

Dig

I could dig deeper into myself, put my head in the sand.
Burrow into the familiar or even into a cave,
But then I would lose sight of the way before me
And I would lose my right to protest or complain.
I cannot allow my silence to become the enemy of truth.
If I care then I will say, if I love then I will do.

I dig deeper into my land and settle into my people,
Choosing to understand both more profoundly,
Because I am living the dream of many millions,
Millions who did not live to see their dream fulfilled,
To see their own return to our homeland.

There was never any choice for me,
Because there was only ever one option,
With no alternative available,
To live in Israel and devote myself to it.

My body would rebel against itself before it would allow me
To go to the desert and bury my head in the sand,
I will not hide myself from life in the Negev,
Nor live forever in the shade,
Waiting until the sun will forgive me.

CURFEW

13.5.21

As days of war passed, the rain of missiles
Shifted to the south and west.
Still close enough to see the explosions from my window,
But far enough away to not have to run for shelter.
Though the sirens had stopped wailing over my home,
They wailed incessantly over the homes of friends and family
Creating a feeling of guilt in the inequality of our suffering.

That night, the residents of our yishuv received a message
From the local municipality, signed by the district police,
A message that brought the terror ever closer to home.
The message stated that groups of neighboring Bedouin men
Had begun blocking the local highways.
They were burning piles of tires and stopping vehicles,
Searching each for Jewish drivers and passengers.
Chaos spread throughout the northern Negev,
The rioting that had begun in Yerushalayim
Had spread to the Negev.

Though they have unrestricted access to the Temple Mount,
The Muslims in Israel were protesting for control of al-Aqsa.
In a time when Israelis were searching for security,
The message we received made all of us wonder,
Who would stop this dangerous chaos from escalating?

They worded it differently, but the interpretation was clear,
The yishuv had instated a curfew for Jews.
They warned us that "due to disturbances"
Residents should remain in their homes,
Do not leave the yishuv after sunset.
The threat of bodily harm showed clearly between the lines.

Local police were overwhelmed with reports
Of people stopped on the highway calling for help.
Piles of tires burned for hours on the highways.
Some residents driving home saw the burning tires
In time and were able to reverse,

But many were stuck in a long line of stopped vehicles.

One father and son from our yishuv, unable to reverse,
Locked the car doors, and the son hid in the backseat.
Masked men walking along the side of the highway
Knocked on widows and checked each car for Jews.
Seemingly all the cars in front of the father and son
Belonged to Arabs or Bedouin because
As they approached the fiery glow of the burning tires
The vehicles in front of them were told to drive on.

When the father pulled toward the pile of burning tires,
The masked Bedouin recognized him as a Jew
And began smashing his windshield and calling for his death.
Instead of seeing the man as a fellow Israeli,
The Bedouin chose to see themselves as Muslim
And the man and his son as Jews.
Manufactured enemies in a baseless conflict.

Through his cracked windshield the Jewish man saw a gap
In the group of masked Bedouin and the burning tires.
Seizing the moment, he accelerated past them,
Saving his life and the life of his son.

Sensitive

14.5.21

Many Jews were able to flee their vehicles,
Flee for their lives in their own homeland,
But several Jews were caught and beaten by Bedouin.

In an interview with Ahmad Alasad, mayor of Lakiya,
One of the largest Bedouin towns in the Negev,
Alasad condemned the "physical violence"
His people enacted on their Jewish neighbors,
But reminded the interviewer that protesting is a legal right.

Alasad said that the Jews of Israel should not be surprised
That the Bedouin are angry and protest the "violence in"
And "mistreatment of al-Aqsa in Jerusalem,
The Muslim's most sensitive holy site."

Reading the interview, the word "sensitive" stood out to me.
I had never heard the word sensitive used about a holy site.
What does "most sensitive" mean in terms of a holy place?
Alasad did not say, "most holy" or "most significant."
So, what did "sensitive" imply?
To me, it implied less of an importance or reverence
For a holy site, but rather a jealous need for control of it.

In the aftermath of the attacks, local residents shared
Their stories and the horrors of seeing their cars burned,
Watching people flee into the dunes, and hearing their cries.
We had been attacked in our own homeland,
Not over some border, but by our own neighbors.

Though it is illegal for Jews to buy land in Bedouin towns,
Bedouin can purchase land in our yishuvim, and many do,
But most prefer to live in a Bedouin town which are not far,
Just walking distance from our yishuvim.
How could this have happened?
How have neighbors become enemies seemingly overnight?

The rumblings had arrived at my doorstep,

And I only had old answers for new questions.
I needed a renewal of truth, new answers for new questions.
And the question foremost in my mind was,
"Why is al-Aqsa a holy site in Islam?"

Wartime passes differently than regular time,
It seems never-ending and there is much time to fill.
I decided to fill mine with learning.
There was plenty of time to learn in the evenings
While living under a curfew for Jews.

HaTikva

Every year on Israel's Independence Day,
An old complaint is complained anew.
Arabs in Israel complain about the exclusiveness
Of Israel's national anthem.
They complain that does not represent all of Israel's citizens
Nor does it reflect all Israeli beliefs.
While Israel is at war against Islamic terrorists
Who call for the destruction of Israel and the death of her Jews,
The complaint this year is more infuriating than other years.

Instead of explicitly condemning all acts of terrorism,
You complain about our national anthem and what it lacks.
You should be assuring your Jewish neighbors
That you are loyal to this country,
To them, and to our shared rights.

In the only democracy in the Middle East,
You are offered a banquet of life choices.
And whatever choice you make it will include
Stipends, subsidies, and scholarships for you.
You could choose to do nothing and still have the right
To vote in all elections and work where you like.

The air in Israel is fragrant with the joy of religious freedom.
Islam in Israel is not confined to its religious spaces,
Rather Islamic prayers float from your minarets
And into Jewish windows five times a day.

And just as sweet is the choice to practice no religion at all,
A choice free of incrimination in Israel.
Freedom of religion here is for both men and women,
But in a country with a national anthem in Arabic,
Most of the women do not have this choice.

And about your religious practice of polygyny,
That results in so many children,
In what other democracy would the law look the other way
And for all your wives and children provide care that is free?

A. E. Hayoun

You and your family receive medical and maternity care,
In the same facilities, by the same Jewish and Arab doctors,
That is provided to the rest of the Israelis.
For each wife you take and each child they bear,
You receive a stipend, money for their care.
There are no requirements for you to receive your share,
We only hope that you spend it on your family's care.

You are given no second, but the best,
The same that is available to me and all Israelis.
And all this from the Jewish country of your complaints.
If it is so terrible in this Jewish state,
Many of you have the option
To live in one of the twenty-two Arab states,
All with anthems that may suit you better.

Though many of their borders are open to you,
Most are all closed to the Jews.
Despite thousands of years of a Jewish presence,
Arab countries have wiped us from their maps,
Denying us our history and any entry.

In Arab countries, there are no Jews to bother you,
But your choices will be fewer and often made for you.
There you will find great opposition
To many democratic freedoms
Especially your choice of who to love
And which religion to practice.
But if your choice is to stay, here in the land of the Jews,
To live as true citizens and enjoy all your rights,
Then exchange your complaints for constructive criticism
And relinquish your hate for support of this state.

In the Jewish state, your life has value
And credence is given to your needs and your voice.
If you and your children wish to live in peaceful equality,
Then your priority must be to stand with Israel,
Unequivocally against terrorism and hatred of the Jew race.
Renounce those among you who support terror regimes,
And loudly declare your support for this country.
Follow the letter of this law and accept no interpretation.

The Camel in the Forest

No matter how much you may complain,
The Jewish state of Israel will remain
Home of the Jews and our anthem unchanged.
Our anthem, our song, declares our unwavering belief
In the Jew's return to their homeland and our hope fulfilled.
We sing our anthem today and carry it with us every day
As free people in our land, Aretz Tzion and Yerushalayim.

A. E. Hayoun

ENOUGH

15.5.21

In the midst of Shabbat,
In the presence of the Shabbat queen,
We celebrate peace, light, and eternity.

We disengage from the world
For one evening to the next.
We turn our questions to prayers
And our actions to thoughts.

But there is one question
That is lucid in our minds
Every day and every night:
How much will be enough?

Of the blood,
The bones,
The children?
How many more
Of my sons, your sons, our sons?

ENEMY

In a small country, the enemy is not far,
But before the war, just a few days ago,
I did not know that the enemy is my neighbor,
Living just a walk from my home,
On the other side of our shared forest.

But they did not appear suddenly,
They were there before the war.
Now that the war has begun,
They simply feel freer
To demonstrate the hate
They had mostly kept hidden
In our daily shared lives.

It may not be all of them,
But the ones who do not hate us
Make no effort to reassure us.
Maybe they are even the majority,
The ones who want peace,
If so, then it is up to them
To show us that peace.

When the neighbor you knew
Becomes the enemy before you,
Everything is changed,
Reluctantly but irreversibly.
It can never be the same again.

And from that change,
A sadness grows slowly
Like a seed planted in darkness
Blooming black in the Negev.

LEARN

16.5.21

To be able to learn again, I erased everything I knew
About Ishmael and Muhammad, Islam and its history.
I was determined to learn the origins and the truth
Of the conflict that has plagued the people of Israel
In their homeland since ancient times.
And my search for answers began with al-Aqsa.

Al-Aqsa is the third most holy site in Islam,
Built on top of the site of the Jewish temple mount during
The Muslim conquest of Jerusalem and Judea after 638 AD.
At the end of his celestial flight from Mecca to Jerusalem,
Muhammad allegedly ascended to heaven at the site of
Haram al-Sharif, the golden-domed mosque at al-Aqsa.

Though Jerusalem is not mentioned in the Qur'an,
Muhammad's unwitnessed journey with the angel Jabreel
From Arabia to the ancient land of Judea in Israel
Was deemed by Muslim's sufficient reason to declare
The holiest place in Judaism, an Islamic holy site.

But before al-Aqsa, Mecca and Medina in Arabia
Were the first holy sites in Islam.
Muslims pray towards the black stone in the Ka'ba at Mecca.
According to Islamic tradition, the Ka'ba was built
By Adam and later restored by Avraham and Ishmael
And then given significance in Islam by Muhammad.

Muhammad built Al-Masjid An-Nabawi in Medina,
Which became the second holy site in Islam.
When Muhammad realized the Jews of Arabia
Would never accept Islam or him as their prophet
He changed the direction of prayer from Jerusalem,
As it is in the Jewish tradition, and instead towards Medina
Where he would later be buried.

I began to read the Quran
And learned the origins of Muhammad's teachings.

The Camel in the Forest

Muhammad received his scriptural revelations
While he was alone in a cave near Mecca.
These revelations would later become the Quran.

But if there were no witnesses with him in the cave
When he received his teachings, then how can his word
Be verified teachings from Allah, from Gd?

For the Jews, nothing of significance has ever occurred
Without Jewish witnesses in their multitudes
To verify the truth of the events, of our history,
And the truth of our Torah received on Har Sinai,
Heard in unison by hundreds of thousands of Jewish ears.

If Muhammad's revelations, and Islam as a religion,
Were created after Judaism and Christianity,
Then Islamic texts, like Christian texts, are based
On the historical and Judaic texts of the Jewish people.
So, how is it that one man's unwitnessed account
Became the basis for a billion-follower religion?

Though I had read the Quran, learned the origins of Islam,
And researched Muhammad, understanding still eluded me.
The connection between the origins of Islam and the reason
For Muslim terrorists launching missiles at me, my family,
And all Israel was tenuous and confusing.

Israel has preserved the heritage sites
And the history of other people who once lived in our land,
Whether they lived here as neighbors or colonizers.
The Muslims have complete access to their holy sites;
Access that often prevents entry for Jews to our holy sites.

If in all major religions, Israel is referred to as
The land of the Jews
But Jerusalem is not mentioned once in the Quran,
And there is no law banning Muslims from holy sites in Israel
Then this conflict is based on something far deeper than greed.
And the much-debated "sensitivity" of al-Aqsa
Can only be a farce used to legitimize hatred of Jewish people.
I had gained understanding, but answers still eluded me.

A. E. Hayoun

INHERITANCE

Isaac and Ishmael, the fathers of two nations,
Were born unto Avraham the father of nations.
Avraham and his wife Sara accepted a covenant
Between Gd and themselves
And became the first Jews, the Ivrim.

The first son of Avraham was Ishmael,
Born of Sara's handmaid, Hagar.
Sara later bore Isaac, her first and only son.
Both Jew and Muslim agree on these two facts,
But agreement diverges as their separate texts continue.

In the Torah, Gd commands Avraham
To send still-pregnant Hagar out to the desert of Paran,
But in the Qur'an, Hajar and Ismail walk willingly to Mecca.
Whether by expulsion or willful leaving,
After Hagar and Ishmael's departure
The Torah and the Quran never converge again.

In Jewish tradition, Hagar cries to HaShem
In the desert at the well Be'er LaHai-Roi.
In Islam, Hajar and her infant Ismail quench their thirst at
The Zam Zam well in the mountains nearby
What would become thousands of years later,
The holy Islamic city of Mecca.

There is one final hint of agreement
Wherein both the Pirkei de'Rabbi Eliezer and the Qur'an
There were meetings between Avraham and Ishmail's wives
Many years after we last hear about Hagar and Ishmael.
Through Avraham and one of Ishmael's wives
Reconciliation is made between father and son.

In both texts, after Sara's death, Avraham marries Keturah,
Allegedly, a secret second name for Hagar meaning fragrant
"Because her deeds were as fragrant as incense."
And of Sara? After her death,
Avraham purchased from Ephron HaHiti

The Camel in the Forest

A cave and the fields surrounding it and buried her therein.

The cave near Hevron and Mamre was named Machpela,
The Cave of the Patriarchs, because therein Avraham,
And all the succeeding patriarchs and three matriarchs,
Were laid there to rest, and it has become a place of return
For the descendants of Avraham and Sara.

In the Qisas al-Anbiya, The Stories of the Prophets,
The reconciliation between Ibrahim and Ismail,
Facilitated by Ismail's wife led them to build the Ka'ba,
The stone building at the center of Mecca
Which later became the holiest site in Islam.

Before he dies, Avraham blesses Isaac endowing him
With all that he owns as well as the inheritance
Of his covenant between Gd and future Jewish descendants.

To his other sons, including Ishmael, Avraham presents
Physical gifts to them and then sends them away,
Eastward, away from Isaac and his inheritance.
But Ishmael returns later and together with Isaac,
They bury their father Avraham in the cave of the Machpela,
Next to his first wife, Sara.

Isaac remained in the land of his father, the land of Israel,
And Ishmael returned to his family in Shur near Egypt.
There he lived out his days with no claim on the lands
Of the Jewish descendants of Avraham,
The Jews of the land of Israel.

A. E. Hayoun

AVUD

Of lost things and their return.
The shattered peace of Shlomo HaMelech,
A splintered kingdom.
The return to erstwhile wrongs,
The avoidance of truth.

Foreign kings and vassal states,
Boiling blood of slain nevi'im.
All was lost and many were slain,
And out of the flames of the Beit Hamikdash destroyed
Our exile was born.

Deep into exile, out into the golah
We carried our traditions and a memory of peace.
Yearning for Beit HaMikdash before its conflagration,
In foreign lands we nurtured a portable yahadut
To nourish our hope for our return to Yerushalayim.

A seventy-year miscalculation of our return from exile,
And our ordained return flouted at Belshazzar's feast.
Mene, Mene, Tekel, Upharsin.
From Darius to Cyrus our suffering lessened.

Ahashverosh and Haman rekindled the flame
Of a burning hatred for the Jews.
But the miracle of Esther's courage saved us in exile.
In 3308, we returned from exile through Esther's son.
Jewish king Darius II allowed us to begin
The reconstruction of our beit hamikdash.

With time's passing, Babylonians replaced Persians.
Our autonomy returned when the count ended
And seventy years had passed
Between the first and second beit hamikdash,
Exactly as foretold.

After exile, the price of our return was the end
Of one thousand years of Jewish prophecy.

The Camel in the Forest

We had returned to Yerushalayim,
But there were none left who could claim,
"So speaks Gd."

But our victory is our return to our homeland
And in our Zionism that was born in the year 3338, not in 5708.
We have returned and continue to return,
Now there are none who can say,
"The Jews have no homeland; in exile they remain."

We have returned to Israel and Judea,
And now we await the arrival of our King
And the restoration of the third Beit HaMikdash.

A. E. Hayoun

WITNESS

A great shofar sounds from within smoke and lightning,
Silencing the nation of Israel at the base of Mount Sinai.
As a nation, the Jews are ready to hear and accept the Torah
And renew their covenant with the God of Avraham.

HaShem descended to the mountain in fire and spoke to us,
To the Jews as a multitude.
Our ancestors were mass witnesses to the presence of God.
We accepted our Torah and it has been enough for us,
Dayenu, for these 3,344 years, and so shall it remain.

In the first century, nearly six hundred years before Islam,
Miriam was alone when the angel Gabriel visited her.
He told her, though an unwed virgin, she would bear a messiah.
In this unwitnessed meeting, Gabriel assured Miriam
That her son was immaculately conceived by Gd.

Miriam's Jewish son Yeshu was born
In the Roman-occupied town of Beit Lechem in Judea.
Yeshu grew up as a Torah-studying, Judaism-practicing Jew.
Yeshu traveled and taught the prophecies he claimed
To have received from Gd and declared himself
The son of Gd and messiah of the Jewish people.

Though Yeshu died before the advent of Christianity,
One of his followers, Shaul, later known as Paul,
Would spread the teachings of Yeshu as a religion for all.
But when Paul realized the Jews would never accept
The idolatrous claim that Yeshu was the messiah,
He blamed the Jews for Jesus's death and determined
That only "faith in Jesus" was necessary to be a believer
And that Judaism in practice had been rendered obsolete.

In the wilderness of Mecca, nearly 600 years later,
While alone in Hira cave, Muhammad received a prophecy.
He was visited by the same angel Gabriel who came bearing
The first verse of the Qur'an, the apparent word of Gd.
Muhammad's solitary revelations of verses of the Qur'an

The Camel in the Forest

Would become the basis of the Islamic religion,
A religion inclusive to everyone who will obey its tenants.

Muhammad and Jesus both believed that they were
The sole prophet, or messenger, of their revelations.
They believed no one could contest (though many did)
A prophecy they alone had each received from Gd.
They both surrounded themselves with believers
Who spent their lives promoting both their teachings.
Some people willingly joined these new religions,
But both religions were spread primarily by colonization,
Conversions of entire people groups under threat and duress.

Though no one was present to verify the truth
Of these two mortal men's prophecies, their followers
Combined now number billions worldwide.
How can it be reconciled that billions of humans
Around the world live, kill, and die by the word of mortal men?

Though both Jesus's and Muhammad's teachings are based
On ancient Judaic texts of witnessed revelations by Gd,
The Bible and the Qur'an simply reinterpreted them
And made their own teachings into addendums.
This supplanting of Judaism gave their prophecies
False validity and created great public discourse
Of their new ideologies,
Discourse that would drive great economic
And political change for thousands of years to come.

The unwitnessed god, the gatekeeping prophet
They demand much from many,
But share little of the truth of their teachings.
They crusade for mass control of the narrative,
Birthing martyrs and zealots in their wake.
And like every influential leader in history,
Their words fueled both political and economic change
Often for the mortal gain of the current leader of the religion.

Despite all the holes in the foundations of these religions,
Billions continue to commit themselves, year after year,
Generation after generation to these mortal men's teachings,
Now patinated by time and accepted as ancient truth.

A. E. Hayoun

In the name of tricky prophets and unwitnessed gods,
The tiny people of Israel have been witnesses to
The destruction of both crusader and colonizer,
And to the irrational demands of the martyr.
For millennia they have come and gone,
Taking and destroying, occupying and expelling.
But they are easily spotted by the Jews of Israel and Judea,
By a people who have witnessed and survived much.

They are still among us, welcomed by us;
Christians in their churches, Muslims in their mosques.
We accept them and support their right to religious choice,
But as I watch Muslim martyrs on the news
Scream for our deaths, I understand
Their goal at Khaybar remains the same.
And in our modern, once ancient, state of Israel,
Now more than ever the Jew must do what is best for the Jew.

WAILING

17.5.21

A wail rises into the cool night air,
Wailing like a baby for milk,
Like cats fighting and mating in the garden,
Like a distorted Gershwin clarinet,
Like the sound of an air raid siren,
And I wake up.

A siren is wailing two streets over, above my son's school.
Rising and falling the sound spreads throughout the yishuv
Rousing all the residents to their bomb shelters.
My beloved is shaking my shoulder,
"Wake up! We must bring the children!"
Though my mind stubbornly remains in a dream
And my eyes are laden heavily with sleep,
My body responds to the coursing adrenaline in my blood.

I run blindly across the cool tile floor to the children's room.
Without a word, I take the baby from his crib,
And their abba takes our eldest from his bed.
With our warm, sleepy children in our arms,
Our adrenaline works like wings,
Taking us in a few bounds from the bedrooms above
To the bomb shelter below.

The bomb shelter is a small low room with an iron door,
Walls of reinforced concrete, filled with unused suitcases
And boxes of winter clothing, there is room for little else.
As we close the door in a rush, the siren fades behind us,
And we are cocooned in the muffled darkness.
Our eldest sits up rigidly in his abba's arms,
Silenced by the siren, his little body alert to potential danger.
Sitting on an old suitcase, I nurse my upset baby into silence.
The weight of myself, my baby, and the milk in my breasts
Feels equal to the weight of the whole universe.

"What about the dog?" I ask in the darkness
"He will hide under the garden stairs;" my beloved answers

"He will be alright." And there is nothing else to say.
And with only sixty seconds to find shelter,
There is nothing else to do.
We sit in silence in the enveloping darkness that smells of
damp underground earth and the sweet scent of children.

The siren continues its circular wail,
And through the concrete walls we hear the interceptions.
Two explosions shake the house above us.
The breath-filled darkness is now warm from our bodies,
Sleep is far from us, quite gone from mind and body.
We sit in silence, thinking the thoughts that only war brings:
"Did our family and friends make it to their shelters?"
Another explosion rattles the door.
"Why do we tolerate these missiles and their hate?"
Our little boy begins to cry.
"What is this world into which we have brought children?"
"The only world there is" comes the answer.

My heart pounds in my chest,
But it is worry that surges through my veins, not fear.
It mixes with my blood to be made into milk
That will nourish my baby through his first year of life.
My feelings flow freely from me to my babies,
I can hold nothing back in the flow of my life-giving milk,
Even if I wish I could.
My milk is tainted, with love, with sadness, joy, and worry,
All the feelings associated with war,
Including hope and courage,
And the most elusive feeling of all: peace.

INDIGENOUS

Who are you, neighbor, cousin?
The world knows us for our differences,
For your great hatred of us,
Despite the enormous amount we have in common.

Many do not wish us to be allies but rather remain enemies,
Pitted for eternity one against the other.
What if we chose to look not at our differences,
But at all that we share; imagine the reality we could create.

So much would need to change to arrive
From the war of here to the peace of there.
The basis of real change is the acknowledgement of truth.
To achieve peace, a deep separation of truth
From your ideologies would have to occur first.

What one chooses to believe does not make it the truth.
Truth is rooted in record and fact and grows into a tree
That blossoms in a spring of understanding
And bears fruit of knowledge and sweet accord
On which we could feast together.

The followers of the Palestinian movement
Would have to acknowledge unreservedly, unironically
Its origins not as a people but as a political movement
Unified under the common goal of the eradication
Of the Jewish state and the Jewish people.

Then the indigeneity of the Jewish people in the land of Israel
Would have to be accepted without exception.
Only thereafter peace and true prosperity could be
The true objective of the Palestinians in the Middle East.

The indigeneity of the Arabs of the Palestinian movement
Is undisputed in the lands surrounding Israel.
Your native lands, both pleasant and fertile,
Are full of the proof of your existence in those countries
Even before Muhammad and his Qur'an.

A. E. Hayoun

They are rich with evidence of your history and culture.

In the ancient kingdoms that once ruled
Lebanon, Jordan, and the Arabian Peninsula,
You flourished in a unique cultural expression,
But those kingdoms, now conquered and colonized
By the single-cultured Islam, can barely remember
Themselves before the contemporary pan-Arab movement.

For a time, your conquest stretched into our land,
You attempted to make Israel and Judea
Part of your Arab conglomerate
When because of decreed exile too few Jews remained.
You entered our land, ruled her,
And made us dhimmis in our kingdoms.

Our land was yours for a time, but despite your declarations,
She was an unwilling lover, loyal only to her own people.
You left your mark on her: minarets, golden domes,
And more Jewish graves, but we returned to her regardless.
We returned to the land where our birthright
Is indelibly imprinted on each grain of sand
And on every mountain and in every valley.

We have accomplished what has seldom been done.
We have reclaimed our land and decolonized her,
Revived our language, and unified our people.
We have returned to our matriarchs in our land.
The Jews have returned home,
And it is time for you to return to yours.

Your lands cry out to you like jilted lovers,
The lands you love less than this "most sensitive" land.
And if you loved this land, you would not wound her
As you do with your missiles and your hate.
Your treatment of this land only proves
That your love is false and your hatred is stronger.

Waste no more time in declaring false indigeneity,
Or in claiming land that is not your own.
Return with pride to your ancient lands,
Write poems of their beauty, visit your abandoned ancestors,

The Camel in the Forest

And then tell me, cousin, tell me your story;
The story of your lands and your people
That I may know them through you
And understand you better.

A. E. Hayoun

SHAVUOT

18.5.21

Gathered together at a festive table,
We experience life again
As it was before our Torah,
When all we had were the laws
That kept us civilized and fed.

We eat dairy foods to remember
The days when we could not eat meat
Until we learned how to slaughter
And cause the least amount of pain;
How to nourish ourselves
And cause the least amount of harm.

On the table is a feast of symbols,
Symbols of our days at Mount Sinai,
Reminders of our willing acceptance
Of the Torah that kept us while in exile,
The Torah that keeps us
In our home returned.

Over the holiday table
A heavy cloth hangs swollen,
Threatening to burst its seams
And its contents ruin our holiday table.
But the threads hold for a while longer,
Long enough to bless this festival,
This day, and the next.

AGREED

Had you agreed you would have your Palestine,
Your Arab utopia in the land of the Jews.
Had you agreed you would have a state
In the Jewish heartland.
Had you simply agreed you would have had then
The land you kill for now.

Had you agreed you would have a state
With any name of your choosing, with a real Arabic name,
Like Ismaelia, Palestine al-Arabiya, or maybe Maqdisia.
It would not have to be a Greek or British Palestine,
A name that only affirms the invention of the Palestinians.
An invented people longing for an invented state.
A making of something from nothing,
The desire to create a state from land
That belongs to another people.

Had you agreed your Arab state on Jewish land,
Given to you by a league of nations, would be legitimate.
Had you agreed you would be advantageously positioned
To wage war on the Jews in the little land left to us.
Had you agreed you would have a military,
And a government to legislate Sharia law
Everything you would need for the state of your dreams.

Had you agreed to the state that has been offered to you,
Everything would be different, for all of us.
But you have declined every offer ever made,
Choosing war over Palestine every time.
You would rather remain false victims for eternity
Than concede that Jews have the right to the land of Israel.

But do not be confused, the Jews do not have Israel
Because of your refusal, not even despite your refusal,
The Jews have Israel because of the miracles,
Many miracles for which we are grateful, despite their cost,
For no miracle comes without its price.

A. E. Hayoun

VAROD

Sister in mauve, woman in pink,
Kindred mother robed in colors of flesh and earth.
Your beautiful, curved eyebrows,
Framed under a paisley-print scarf,
Shade your watchful eyes that watch your sons
As they play with my sons on the same playground.

We are close enough to smile and chat,
But there is a distance between us,
And I am not sure of its extent,
But it feels too great to cross at the park.
Sitting here together but separate at the park,
We don't have to smile,
We could just start with "Shalom."

Though it seems we don't have much in common,
If we only look for it, there must be more that we share,
Especially as mothers to sons.

We could share our favorite recipes,
Cups of tea, and our sister languages.
We could walk together on worn forest paths,
With our boys or just us two.
We might discover shared experiences
Or realize how well we understand
Each other's culture, better than any other can.

We could talk about our mothers, the ancient and the new,
Or remember our father Avraham.
Though we've been given two different inheritances,
We are here now, living together in this land.
I believe in our commonality and the good it can achieve,
If only we would choose to see it.

PAWN

A player of the smallest size and value.
A person used for the purpose of others.
The Palestinians in the Middle East.
These three things are the same,
And those who do not see it are the ones screaming
From both ends of the horseshoe,
Themselves a pawn of a different kind.

The worlds cries, "Free Palestine," "Genocide in Gaza,"
"Palestinian Ethnic Cleansing," "Israel Apartheid,"
But they know little of Israel, Palestine, or apartheid,
And even less about Palestinian oppression
At the hands of their own Arab brothers.

When Yehuda, Shomron, and Jerusalem were ruled
By Jordan's King Hussein II, why was Palestine not created?
Why were the Arabs of British Mandate Palestine
Left in a refugee state when they could have had a state?
Who stands to benefit from these Palestinian refugees?

The protester, the screamers, the Jew-haters,
They don't want to know that it was Israel
Who brought water and civil services to Jerusalem in 1967,
They won't hear of Israel as home to millions of Arabs,
And they don't care that Muslims have equal rights in Israel.

They will never blame an Arab country or leader
For the plight of the Palestinians,
They continue to ignore the truth so they can blame the Jews.

But how different all our lives would be
If the world would choose to accept the truth
About who treats the Palestinians like humans
And who treats them like pawns.

A. E. Hayoun

SHAWATI

We sat in exile
On the banks of the Dijlah,
Singing songs of love for our home.
By the rivers of Babylon, we sat and wept
For our Israel, distant in exile.

Cast into exile
And cast out again,
Told to return to our home.
We have left exile behind.

They drove us away
From the Dijlah and al-Furat,
And we carried with us
The memory of them in song and shir
To the banks of the Yarden.

On the banks of the Yarden
We sat and wept for a while.
Tears for the homes lost,
Tears for the home returned.

We settled happily
Near the banks of the Yarden,
Reunited with our Yerushalayim,
And returned to our Negev and Galil.

Restored to our home,
Returned to our prayers,
But little time passed
Before they came to us saying,
"You've stolen this home,
Go back from where you came."

And then we knew
That they speak without thought
And hear without ears.

The Camel in the Forest

To them our story, our history
Is inconsequential and easily erased.

We answered them, our words
Like ripples from two rivers,
"Here is our home, here in this land.
From one river to the next
And back again, we have returned
And in this our home, we are free."

But even as the truth washed over them,
They stared at us unblinkingly with a hardened gaze,
Hard as the stones along two rivers.
Their answer is:
"We only want you gone from this home and the next."

A. E. Hayoun

Conqueror

Cast out and exiled, left to wander the Earth,
Murdered in our millions, and denied entry to our land.
For too long the Jews were the conquered,
Our Israel colonized, falsely apportioned,
And brazenly renamed by those who had no right to it.
Yet they did not hesitate to claim the right of conqueror.

The Jews returned to their land, our home we reclaimed,
Not without hostile contempt and great sacrifice.
World powers conceded the right of Jews to return to their land,
And when Arab nations waged war against us,
Our victory over them only confirmed our right to our land.
Though we received this land by right, by gift, and by victory,
We are still denied the rights of conqueror.

While the world delays its judgment of our enemies,
They hold us to a different standard.
They insist we prove our morality is greater,
And show mercy to those who showed no mercy to us.
We are forced to make provisions for our murderers,
When we have undeniable rights as the conqueror.

Despite every reason to be decisive, our politicians hesitate.
They bend to the strong winds that blow ever from the West.
Unwilling to lose their seat or risk their importance,
They hesitate to act for the greater good of Israel.
Why do they fear the judgment of others?
For as long as the treasonous live among us
And unchecked are the shouts of the anarchists,
In hesitating to silence them, the Jewish homeland is at risk.
We did not steal this land; we are not the colonizers,
Therefore, to us every right as the conqueror.

Under radical Islamic leadership,
Poorly disguised as the Palestinian Authority,
There is no future for the Arabs or the minorities they govern.
Their government's goal is not peace or even a state,
They have declined it all before and will do so again.

The Camel in the Forest

Radical Muslims may change their minds about a state,
But they will never change their means to that end,
Believe them when they say
They want statehood and kill the Jews too.
Still the world expects Israel to extend the offer again,
Give up our land to those who wish us dead.
We have no reason to consider a two-state solution
When in our land, we have every right as the conqueror.

To the conqueror the right to prioritize its citizens,
Ensure they are safe without a thought of who it offends.
To the conqueror the ability to legislate the difference
Between lawful free speech and prosecutable treason.
To the conqueror the right to defend their country,
And determine who is an ally and who is an enemy.
To the conqueror the right to wage war or make peace.

From weakness and hesitation, precarious peace is born,
Leaving room for interpretation and exploitation of the law,
Laws that should function as shields to protect the citizens.
For any Jewish homeland worth having,
Israel must have the right of the conqueror.

A. E. Hayoun

LEVAVOT

19.5.2021

How does one teach children about war?
What can the smallest child understand of hatred and death?
I instruct my young children that they must run to me
If they hear a siren while we play in the garden.
I search their faces for agreement or acknowledgement
But the call of bugs and beetles from the spring grass
Is louder in their ears than my instruction.
They giggle and writhe in my arms waiting
To be freed into the pleasures of the afternoon sun.

As the children play, I also take the time to enjoy the garden.
Sitting in the grass, I allow the sunlight
To soften the muscles of my face and darken my skin.
Scant clouds ripple and skip in the windy shamayim,
But my enjoyment of them ends when I see
White trails like shooting stars streak across the sky.
I cannot hear them or the sirens that warn of them
But their vibrations ripple the air as they pass overhead.

As distant sirens wail in Be'er Sheva,
And I sense the fleeing feet of thousands seeking shelter,
My heart clenches as I remember that my husband
Was meant to work in Be'er Sheva today.
Working from building plans in unfinished structures,
He is exposed in buildings with no windows, no doors,
And no place to shelter, just concrete shells of buildings
That can crumble like paper under missile impact.

Though only twenty minutes away by car,
Be'er Sheva now seems a world away from
The current safety of my sunny garden.
My heart skips a beat, two, and then many.
A tightness begins to spread through my chest,
A tightness that has become familiar these days.
I tell myself that he will find shelter, he must find shelter,
But regardless, my heart abandons its steadfast work
And I feel it rush towards Be'er Sheva

The Camel in the Forest

To look for our lover and learn he is safe.

No more than a few minutes have passed since
I saw the missiles flying overhead,
But it takes all my power to stop myself from calling him,
A phone call that would only distract him
From finding shelter, and he must find shelter.
I count the explosions above Be'er Sheva,
But I stop counting as the sixth explosion shakes
The ground across the Northern Negev;
The vibration of a direct hit.

Little white specks dance in my vision
Reminding my heart that it must resume its
Promised work of creating blood from breath
Regardless of the unknown fate of my husband.
Unfazed by the knowledge of war's realities,
My sons continue joyfully digging for treasures in the dirt.
I watch through the dancing white specks in my eyes
And beneath furrowed brows as the white trails of missiles
Begin to fade into the clouds above.
My heart returns to its steady beating
And with it a quiet understanding that
If my heart is still beating then my husband must be safe,
Or surely my heart would not have returned at all.

I close my eyes and let the sun soften my face again
Counting a few minutes more until I dial his number
And wait for an answer.
After a few unanswered rings, the dancing white specks
And tightness in my chest threaten to return,
But they dissipate as soon as I hear him,
Shouting out of breath, "Ani beseder, mami, hakol beseder."
He had been on the sixth floor of an open building
And took shelter with others behind a stack of cinderblocks.
They watched through an opening in the concrete walls as
A missile hit the ground in the open desert across the street.
Later, on his drive home, sirens would sound again.
He and others on the highway would stop their vehicles
And run to lie flat in the sand alongside the road
As the Iron Dome would intercept missiles over their heads.

A. E. Hayoun

At the end of the day, he did come home to me,
And in the garden my arms encircled him,
Pressing his dust-covered warmth into me.
While I made dinner, he showered off the dust of the day
And washed down the drain the dusty evidence of war.
As we eat dinner in the garden, enjoying the cool evening air,
For a moment life feels like it had before the war.
Bright and clean, satisfying and warm.
How quickly everything has changed after a few days of war.
The sun sets in the garden, purple pervades the evening air,
And I cry for the mothers, the lovers, and all the children.

APARTHEID

O apartheid,
How cruel and untrue.
Like stones, they hurl you at this land
Hoping to crush it under your weight.

O apartheid,
They who throw you are diverse in company
But unified in the motive of their lies:
Destroy the Jews, take their land.

O apartheid,
How exhausting it must be,
To have your definition so disregarded,
To be made to represent that which you don't define.

O apartheid,
You are not alone.
You can find similar company
In "segregation," "colonizers," and "genocide."
They too have suffered abusage in excess.

O apartheid,
They know nothing about this country.
If they did, they would know
That you do not relate to reality here.

O apartheid,
They defiantly choose to ignore
Your truth and the truth of this land.
There is nothing here to make you stay.

So, apartheid, I will tell you good-bye
From the land of your antonym,
From the antiapartheid.

A. E. Hayoun

UGANDA

"Lama lo Uganda?" Why not Uganda?
If the slogan used for a Jewish Palestine in Uganda
Was good enough for us, why isn't it good enough for you?

The Zionist dream was nearly given a chance in Uganda,
Many Jews considered it a viable option.
If we could have a place in the world,
For all Jews to live at peace with the world,
Then we were willing to consider giving up our homeland.

An idea of the British colonizer's invention,
The people of Uganda did not make the offer.
Had they been given the choice I'm sure
They would not have agreed to give up their land
To establish an African Jewish homeland.

But to the Jews who survived a genocide,
Any offer of a safe homeland was an offer worth considering.
Jews were willing to give up their ancestral lands,
The cornerstone of Zionism, our return to Eretz Yisrael,
Because the idea of freedom in a land of our own
Mattered more than "winning."

So why has no such offer been made for Palestine?
Why has no offer been made for Palestine in another land,
Perhaps one from which the Palestinians have heritage?
Though there are no Palestinian artifacts in the land of Israel,
But there is much evidence of the Palestinian's Arab origins
In the surrounding Arab countries from which they came.

So why must Palestine be created on Jewish land,
Why is that a required condition for peace?
When in fact, a two-state solution already exists,
The British Mandate of Palestine was divided in two,
Forty percent became Israel and sixty percent Jordan.
So why is there no demand for a free Palestine in Jordan?
Why at the very least won't Jordan absorb the Palestinians,
Or Egypt and Lebanon make provisions for them?

The Camel in the Forest

If it was acceptable in the world for hundreds of years
To scream at the Jews in the diaspora,
"Go back to where you came from!"
Then why can't the same be respectfully said
To the Arabs in Israel who yearn for Palestine?
Is it a double standard or just taboo because they aren't Jews?

Why has no offer of land for Palestine been made?
Why do Palestinians need help from foreign aid?
Is it because the entire Arab Middle East
Does not believe that Palestine should exist?

Since they have declined every offer of statehood,
Perhaps the Palestinians should just admit that they
Don't want a state as much as they don't want Israel to exist.
They want the Jewish state or none at all.
They want Israel or the Palestinians be damned.

If the direct descendants of King David can consider,
Even as a possibility, giving up their Jerusalem
For the sake of saving their children and their people,
Then surely the Palestinians, born of the 20th century,
Can find another piece of land for their Palestine.

Why doesn't the world look to Arab leaders
To help create this elusive Palestine, this exclusive Arab state?
If the Palestinians want their own country,
They should stop blaming their troubles on the Jews
And instead, ask themselves, "Lama lo Uganda?"

A. E. Hayoun

FREEDOM

Blue on blue.
Identities
Framed in blue.

Rights to vote
For our choice,
Rights to work
Where we choose.

Blue cards
To speak our minds,
Blue cards
For freedom or treason.

My card in my purse,
Yours in your pocket.
The same rights,
The same opportunities.

Blue cards
Of the Jewish state.
How will we use them,
For good or for evil?

It depends
How much we value
The freedoms of this blue state
An island in a sea of red autocracy.

BEDOUIN

Who is the colonizing monster that hides in plain sight,
Fooling Europe and the West because "colonizers are white"?
Where are the flags of the SWANA minorities?
Their bright colors replaced with pan-Arab-colored authority.

Which minority marches willingly towards ethnocide?
The Bedouin in the Negev,
They have begun to choose Palestinian suicide.

There are Bedouin who have achieved the impossible,
They have left their childhood tents and become unstoppable.
We are grateful to those who have served this country,
They are not required to but do so proudly.

Their doctors and lawyers represent a respected minority,
but those Bedouin are not the majority.
Bedouin of the Negev, Israeli as the rest,
The Bedouin in Israel are putting their loyalties to the test.

They are trading their freedoms in a democracy,
For a place among the Palestinians and false new identity.
Instead of living freely as Israelis in their Bedouin traditions,
They will be required to adhere to the terrorist's conditions.

United together under Sharia law, the Bedouin begins to fade
And will be replaced with a tool for terror in an unfair trade.
The Palestinian cause is just a cog in the machine,
A tool to kill Jews in the great pan-Arab colonizer scheme.

Once the Bedouin will have traded freedom for a false ideal,
It will be too late to return their loyalties to Israel.
They will be threatened if they try to return to life as it was,
Because there is no leaving the Palestinian cause.

Their only choice is to embrace the error
And sacrifice everything in support of Palestinian terror.
They will learn quickly to accept all forms of crime and rape
As necessities for pan-Arabism acquiring another false state.

But there will come a day when their grandfathers praise
The tenuous peace with the Jews and long for those days.
From the deception of terrorism, there is no departure,
No escape from fading Bedouin and expendable martyr.

AL-NAKBA

Al-Nakba for dhimmi laws, our lost sudra, and every pogrom.
Al-Nakba for the Inquisition, the Holocaust, and Khaybar.
Al-Nakba for the Crusades, al-Farhud, Giado, and Babi Yar.

Al-Nakba for the Alexandria riots,
For millennia of antisemitism.
Al-Nakba for every lost ghetto and shtetl,
For every Jewish victim of terror and rape.
Al-Nakba for every murdered Jew,
For every home we were driven from.

Al-Nakba for every Jewish quarter destroyed,
For every holy tomb defiled.
Al-Nakba for every Jewish catastrophe
And we would never stop commemorating.
Al-Nakba for every Jewish death
And we would never stop weeping.

Al-Nakba, al-Nakba,
You should have agreed to Resolution 181,
But instead, you started a war you thought you couldn't lose.
And in that gamble, you lost
The opportunity for peace, and your homes too.

Al-Nakba, al-Nakba,
What did you expect would happen?
You would win against the eternal Jew,
Keep your homes and take ours too?
You didn't bet on peace because you thought
The hated Jews would just lay down and die?

No, al-Nakba, we are not Jews with trembling knees.
Keep your al-Nakba and honor your loved ones,
But don't ever believe your al-Nakba was because of the Jews.

A. E. Hayoun

GVULOT

20.5.21

What are borders if they are open not closed?
Closed borders close us to our land,
Open borders open our land to murderers.
Closed, not open, borders must remain closed.

When I could remain indoors no longer,
Shut away from war and the world,
I left through the front door and ran to the hills.
My feet followed familiar paths,
But my breath was out of practice.

I passed Hiran, my unchanged friend,
And walked to the edge of the forest.
The nearby checkpoint provides its illusion of security,
But just beyond it, east along the border,
The hole in the sagging security fence is absurdly accessible.

Overlooking Yehuda and Shomron,
Standing at the top of the hill,
I watched the gaping mouth before me,
A hole in the border torn open
By greased shears and strong hands.

I saw them before they saw me,
Thirty or so cousins crawling boldly
Out of the mouth in the broad light of day.
When they saw me, they stopped and stood,
And we all stood staring, waiting for something to happen.

At the edge of the mouth, we all seemed to forget
Who was standing on the lips and who on the tongue.
Who was being spat out and who was being swallowed?
Which of us would throw the first stone?
Which of us could?

VOTE

When you vote, do you vote for us all?
For those of us who live in the South,
For the Jews both near and far?
Do you vote for the Jews who look like you
And for the ones who don't?
Do you vote for the lives of those beyond the center,
Beyond your center?
Because it seems that for many, your center is Tel Aviv,
But for the rest of us, its Yerushalayim.

We have already abandoned Rachel,
Limited our time with Sara, Rivka, and Leah,
And we are losing the fight to save Joshua's altar.
We are already wary of visiting many of our ancestral lands
For fear of stoning or death.
So how much more are you willing to surrender
For the false peace Tel Aviv, that daydream splendor?

How much more land are you willing to give up
For that elusive two-state solution
With those who don't want your peace?
Another piece here, another piece there.
Like food to a stray dog never satisfied
It will always take more than it can consume,
Only to vomit it up and then bite the hand that fed it.

We have compromised, given much for little in return,
And like the stray dog, they return to blame us
For their wreckage, their flawed society, and all that they lack.
But they return regardless, and they always demand more.
If they demand Jerusalem for their Palestine
What makes you think they won't demand Tel Aviv too?

For a while, your center will be safe,
But if they have their way
They will have Yerushalayim and Tel Aviv too.
So, before you sell the bones of your mothers
To try and keep the city of your desires,

Listen carefully to their chant,
"From the River to the Sea" ends with Tel Aviv.

CEASEFIRE

Silly ceasefire like a game played with children
Who cry when the rules don't work in their favor.
Every time Israel is attacked, it is forced to play
The ceasefire game of the aggressor's invention
With rules that change as the game plays on.

But war is not a game and terrorists are not children.
Islamic terrorists are members of a death cult
Who indoctrinate their children to be suicidal martyrs.
After they have started a war with Israel,
They scream for a ceasefire when they run out of resources.
Then to gain world support, they change their narrative
From murdering terrorist to misunderstood minority.

For Islamic terrorists who don't care about their citizens,
A ceasefire is not a humanitarian pause but a time to reload.
While they plan their next attack,
They use the ceasefire to gain control of the media narrative.
The Palestinians bring out their dead dolls and fake blood,
To put on the performance that earns them billions of dollars
In the foreign aid that keeps their façade standing
In the rubble of their legitimacy.

With Hamas as their elected government,
The Palestinian majority rejects every offer of peace
In exchange for a purgatory of false identity.
How can a peace agreement ever be reached
With a group of people whose ideology is death?

Where does that leave us? What choice does Israel have?
Until the day arrives when Palestinians will choose
Life over death and peace with the Jews,
Elohim Gadol v'am Yisrael chai.

A. E. Hayoun

SHOFET SHOCHET

The shofet shochet, butcher of justice
Robed in human rights, only camouflaged injustice.
The greatest threat to the Jewish right to exist
Is the shofet shochet, not the next terrorist.

Our judges watch the terror unfold
Citizens murdered, the trauma untold.
But our judges determine the life value is greater
Not for the victim, but for the perpetrator.

If a world is saved when you save a Jewish life
Then for a Jew's death, what is the price?
In tax-payer prisons, terrorists languish for a lifetime,
But there is no amount of time that will atone for their crime.

With foreign donations to the Palestinian cause,
Hamas pays terrorists who have broken all fundamental laws.
They are "pay-to-slay" hires with blood on their hands,
But our judges repeatedly decide to release them back into our lands.

Terrorists bid and rest until their day of release,
When they can murder anew, their intent will never cease.
There is no end, no peace in sight,
Until our judges understand, it must be a life for a life.

Are the Jews murdered by Ahmed worth any less
Than the Jews murdered by Eichman? Tell me, confess.

No excess of humanity toward terrorists can atone,
For the Jewish lives lost, forever etched in stone.

Safe in our homeland, we have naught to prove,
So, is justice only for others, but not for the Jews?

"Every life has value" is our firm belief,
But to wage a war against those who do not share this belief,
How can we win? What can we achieve,

The Camel in the Forest

When our judges betray us and murderers are set free?

We fight for justice with lives we cannot justify
But their losses and ours they only glorify.

Do not make me consider, as a proud Israeli,
That if terrorists in Israel were tried under sharia law,
Would the outcome be more just? Maybe.

Shofet shohet, you are responsible for the next victim's fate,
Make the right decision before it is too late.
The solution is simple, Israelis want trial without error,
To live free in full knowledge of life without terror.
Do your duty unto your people, weigh and pronounce
Do not hesitate in justice, and truth do not denounce.

Until our judges understand that we cannot afford
For them to think otherwise, nor this question be ignored:
I ask my fellow Jews, "Is it the murdering terrorist
Who threatens the Jews in Israel and our right to exist?
Or is our greater threat,
The shofet shohet?

A. E. Hayoun

End

21.5.2021
After twelve nights of watching the blue and orange box
Of the Homefront Command in the corner of the tv screen
Update names of cities in Israel under missile fire,
The endless shuffling of names has ceased with a ceasefire.

After twelve days of war, a ceasefire was agreed upon.
But to what end? Lives were lost for nothing,
And no greater peace or security was achieved.

This useless ceasefire will only ensure
Hamas will be better prepared for their next attack.
This futile end will only prolong the cycle of terror
And risk more innocent lives in the years to come.

By the war's end, 4,360 missiles had been launched at Israel,
Of which 3,573 penetrated Israeli airspace.
Even with the Iron Dome's high interception rate,
357 missiles entered Israel, killed, and caused damage.

And the remaining 780 missiles launched from Gaza?
Some fell into the sea but the majority backfired into Gaza,
Killing and wounding Gazan civilians.
Civilian deaths that will never be reported
Or only falsely reported as caused by Israeli airstrikes.

So now it begins, a new cycle of a tenuous peace
Sure to be shattered again in the not-too-distant future.
Inevitably, terrorists in Gaza will break the ceasefire
And the world will again turn against Israel for its self-defense.

Israelis are just expected to accept this reality,
But how can we ever sleep peacefully
When just over the fence thousands of murderers
Are just waiting for the next opportunity?

MEMORIAL

To the memory indelible of those we have lost.
For those cut down in youthful defense of our country.
For those who fell seeking shelter from hateful missiles.

For those who have lost someone before
And been made to remember their loss anew.
For those whose grief has stolen their words.

For the fallen and their families,
Their children born and unborn,
For the lives lived and yet to be lived.

We will remember you
And your memory will be a blessing.

In memory of the thirteen victims of terror z"l who were murdered during Operation Guardian of the Walls and for their families who must survive without them.

A. E. Hayoun

BALFOUR

But they won, really.
The colonizers, the British.
Though we hate to admit it,
They have won.

They never wanted us to be united,
Never wanted us to live as the children of Avraham.
They came and turned us
One against the other.

But given the chance on our own,
We may have stood a chance, together.

Even after they have gone, as it is now,
We cannot agree on anything,
Except being the children of Avraham.

AL-AQSA

The dust has settled,
The missiles have ceased,
The fires are put out,
But there is no peace.
The bitterness of war lingers on our tongues.

Al-Aqsa still stands; the third-most holy site in Islam.
The "most sensitive" holy site,
Still not mentioned in the Qur'an.

Despite the ceasefire, the "innocent" Palestinian civilians
Are still launching missiles from Gaza towards al-Aqsa,
A site so important and holy to them,
They threaten to destroy it.

The Muslims in Israel continue to riot inside al-Aqsa,
Barricade themselves in, armed with homemade explosives,
Desecrating the interior of their third-most holy site.

The rioting may continue for a long time to come,
But their riots are not considered incitement to war,
They are simply a reality of everyday life in Israel.
And the Israelis are expected to accept it.

Though al-Aqsa was deliberately built on top
Of the Jewish Temple Mount during the Arab occupation,
Even today, Jews are only allowed to enter the grounds
A few days a year to recite special prayers that are indivisible
To the physical location of the Temple Mount in Jerusalem.
The same Jerusalem and Temple Mount
That are mentioned over seven hundred times in Judaism.

Even when our entry days arrive,
We are often prevented from entering,
Sometimes by rioters, but more often by our own leaders.
Our leaders give in to the loud cries of the Palestinians
Instead of protecting the rights of the people they serve.

If the leaders of the Jewish nation are swayed by the loudest
Then perhaps the Jews need to be louder still.
The war is over but there is no denouement.
The war is over but it will never end.
The war is over and I return to the forest.

LOVE

Because all the good still lies before me.

A. E. Hayoun

WAKE

After war, afterward.
After such little time, so much has changed.
Inside and outside, open and closed.

Open palms have become closed fists.
Sands have settled; all have shifted.
With furrowed brow, neighbor faces neighbor.

The dukhifat still cries at nightfall.
I am still moved by shirat hadekel.
Some things have not changed.

War has left and what it has left behind
Is everything I know and nothing I recognize;
Life distorted in a strange light like the world before dawn.

Peace has tried to return to the Negev.
I watch its approach and hear its moaning voice
Like a wounded animal seeking refuge or death.

War has left. I have sent peace on its way.
I tread new paths in the Negev
And streaming in my wake is a trail of broken glass
Reminding me of next year in Yerushalayim.

Though glass cuts my feet and wind deafens my ears,
I set out resolute, stumbling across the dunes,
Finding my desert legs again.

I push past my fearful understanding of the Negev,
And search anxiously to recover lost time.

GONE

Nearly a year has passed
Since I have seen them,
My camels.

The camels are gone,
They left with the war
And have not returned.

I have driven into the desert
In passionate search of them,
Climbed over foothills
Into the shade of the pines,
But my camels are gone.

I return to where they were.
I wait for a while
In the dunes, near the caves,
But the camels do not return.

My eyes scan the horizon
From each window of my house,
Searching for the camels I knew so well.

They must have borrowed the wings
Of the hasida or the livnit and migrated
Away for the summer, or possibly forever.

Or maybe from the choled they learned how to burrow,
Using their long necks to dig deep into the desert,
Past the sands, into Yabbasha.

I thought they would stay with me,
But the camels are gone.
And I know they have gone away with the war.

A. E. Hayoun

Memory

As I water the garden, the roses and jasmine,
A blast shakes the neighborhood.
It's just an exploded powerline transformer.
It's nothing. Everything is fine.
But my breath is short and my chest is tight.

Finally asleep, resting at last,
Yet I wake throughout the night
With sweaty palms and the prickle of pins
Caused by the distant explosions of military drills.

War has retreated, life has returned,
But the rumblings and shaking
Still reverberate throughout Israel.

We have moved forward,
Maybe our minds have moved on,
But our bodies keep their own score.

FEAR

An ancient beast, both strange and familiar,
Has begun to terrorize the Negev.
Its shaggy, matted head emerges from a lair in the forest.
The beast has grown old since I last saw it,
Grown old at last.

Dripping old sweat and fresh blood
From self-inflicted wounds,
It follows behind my steps in the Negev.
Fear returned brings fear itself,
A tiresome beast stalking the Negev in daylight.

Burrowing out of the ground,
It hides in shadow and cave.
There can be no return to the forest,
No return to familiar paths in the desert for me
If the beast will remain in the Negev.
If I am to return then this beast must be killed.

Hot in the desert, I stand facing a cave.
Like a great mouth, it lies open before me,
The ancient lintel jagged like broken teeth.
I throw no stones to scare out the foxes,
I know it is no fox that lurks inside that cave.

I step over the threshold and blindly enter the darkness,
A pervasive stench hangs from the stone walls.
Stepping over scattered boulders,
I step deeper into the fetid gloom.
Familiar black soot spreads like a cloud across the ceiling,
But it isn't soot, it's the presence of fear.

Ragged breath, thick with damp and saliva,
Wafts over me from the depths of the cave.
I hear its overgrown claws scraping
And its matted body shaking,
Reverberating around the walls of the cave.

A. E. Hayoun

Like choking smog and a thunderclap,
The beast is at my throat,
Smothering me, choking me.
My ringing ears hear nothing but a fearful whine.

My arms flail at their greatest extent,
Searching for something with which to strike the beast.
Pulled from the sand at my side,
A jagged piece of flint, like a knife in my hand,
Splits open its skull.

The beast is too old and too slow to have this victory.
With its last breath,
Its presence retreats, its stench dissipates,
And the cave is left silent.

I drag the carcass out into the sunlight.
Exposed in the hot sand it is pitiful and ugly,
A scrawny body falsely enlarged
By the fear that surrounded it.

I call to the birds, to the nesherim circling above,
They swoop and glide, falling through the sky
To land on the ground beside me.
Their throats undulate as their lizard eyes meet mine,
They understand my wordless command.

I turn my back and walk away
From the sounds of tearing fur and picking at flesh.
I leave the vultures to finish the work
Of devouring the remains of the beast
And expunging fear from the Negev.

OTEF

Lay me upon your formations,
Wrap me in your folds and strata.
Bring me into your caverns, into your ancient wells.
Let me enter your dwelling places
And breathe deeply your musk of extinguished life.

Profound was my love of earth and stone,
But until I walked your ruined places,
I did not know that love could reverberate.

When the early rains streak your face,
And both earth and stone are wet and cold,
You soften and shift, crumple and contract
Until you divulge long-hidden stones and secret relics.

In the second spring in the Negev,
I climb muddy hills and seek out your painted treasures
Thrilling at their sight,
I wrap them in canvas and take them home.

When marauders haunt your ruined gardens
Leaving refuse in your hidden caves,
I gather it back, sort it, and curse it.

When they are absent, I am present,
Walking your paths, and singing to the trees.
Your rugged simplicity, your natural beauty
Call me back time and again.

A day will come when you crush me with your earth,
Cover me with your sands,
And weigh me down with feldspar and dolomite
Keeping my bones as my soul takes flight.

A. E. Hayoun

CLEAN

Sand trickles into the sulci of my mind
Piling up into dunes that reach
The ceiling of my thoughts.

In this desert, home to creatures
No stranger than myself,
They spend their time burrowing
And I take the time to excavate myself.

I know the desert, and it knows me.
In the desert, daydreams and reality
Meld together like a mirage.

At the sun's center,
All dreams and desires pulsate,
Warming blood and bone,
Turning hairs from brown to gold.

In distant mountains,
A place of purple fire is suspended
Beneath a dry blue sky filled with wings
That fly between heaven and earth.

Standing in the golden desert,
In the silence of heat and light,
The path before me is darkened
With painted ore and shadows long.
Here everything is serene;
Everything in the desert is clean.

Prahim

From water grows flowers.
I give water, I am given flowers.

Life is as simple as that.

And yet, life leads us to forget that
From water grows flowers.

A. E. Hayoun

MAGIC

They showed me the Negev and I left myself there.
They told me of its scars and ruin,
But I filled them with gold and stacked fallen stones.
They told me the desert is an arid wasteland,
But I found beautiful flowers and magical fauna.

They said it would be difficult
To learn the language of this land,
Now I speak its legends and sing its blessings.
I am here, and if I were anyone else,
Would the Negev know me?

All that plagues you I have kissed and caressed.
You give me oranges and anise,
I bake cakes and drink flavorful arak.
I have made a home in this desert,
But I do not ask it to bloom.

Others see you through a window of conflict
But I stand within your vortex of magic.
They told me we wouldn't last,
Now I sleep in your dunes and laugh with your winds.

Many arrived to meet you and then could not wait to leave,
But since they showed you to me,
I have not looked away since.

CONSTANT

When there is nothing new under the sun,
When all matter has been transformed
From new to known to new again,
Reality becomes cyclical
And change is just a return.

The desert I now know teems with creatures
Once hidden to me but now well-known.
Snails sleep beneath the sands,
Hot days turn to damp, cool nights,
And camels sleep in the forest.
But it was all there before me.

The hate that blazes towards Israel
Returns in yearly revolutions
Like the turn of the Earth around the sun.
Each generation feels its heat,
But it did not begin when it began for us.

I have come to anticipate continual change,
Like the fluctuating temperatures of spring in the Negev,
Change has become the only true constant.
I ride its currents as trusting as a swallow on the wind.

I used to resist change and regret leavings
But time has taught me that it exists only in the present.
I may hold on to my familiar life in the Negev
But the trucks rumble through and the foxes seek new burrows
I can resist the change, but much will change regardless,
So, instead of making love under the circumstances
I am making love under the palm trees.

A. E. Hayoun

GOLEM

Deep within the desert,
In a cave sunk into the face of a cliff,
I lay inert, wrapped in linen, and caked in mud,
I, the golem in the desert geniza.

My purpose awaits me at the base of the cliffs,
But the Aleph eludes me and I remain *met*.
Beside me in piles, half-covered in sand,
Lay ruined scrolls of broken words and malformed prayers.
In this desert attic, I am captive,
Smothered under the weight of Jewish mistakes,
Foreign judgement, and forgotten strength.

A song floats up from the desert below,
It blows south on the wind from Hevron.
A melody whistles through all the caves,
It rustles like wind through solitary palms.
I awaken, encased in old linen and new mud,
And begin consuming letter, scroll, bandage, and cloth
Metabolizing them into courage and truth
That fills my mouth and stops my words.

Now the cave is empty and I am parched,
All that is left is the Aleph near my feet.
The dried mud on my joints cracks and splits as I rise.
I take up the Aleph and place it as a crown upon my head.
My encasement of mud chips and breaks,
Falling from me in sheaves
Shattering at my feet like pieces of pottery.

Standing within the cave, I stare at the entrance,
Out towards Edom, towards the new sunlight.
I crawl to the edge of the opening,
Fearful of falling down the sheer rocky face,
But then I remember: I can fly.
Looking out over the Negev, I spread all my wings:
The two covering my face, the two covering my feet,

The Camel in the Forest

And the two on my back with which I take flight.

From the desert attic, I fly into the sunlight,
Shining in my purpose as queen of the desert,
Metamorphosing sand into gold,
Wind into song,
And death into truth.

A. E. Hayoun

HEAVENS

The clouds are shaped like the Aleph-Bet.
The sun ring of daylight and the moon's penumbra
Hold wild dreams in their infinite circles.

Staring at the blue Negev sky
The blood behind my eyes shimmers
And my hair dances above my head.

The sky above the desert is full
Of the watchful eyes of migrating birds.
From their feathery wings fall the scents
Of African steppes and Eurasian snow.
They watch me from the heavens.

As the angels, stars, and celestial bodies
Twinkle and glitter as they determine the seasons,
Set the time, and create light and night,
I wonder if they know why.

From season to season, I watch them above me
And wait for them to give me an answer,
To tell me what they know,
Of why we are here in heaven and on earth.

IMAOT

Rahel, I love you. At your roadside, I call to you.
Leah, I miss you. At your cave, I breathe your scent.
Sara, is that you, shining in the darkness?
Rivka, do you know me? I think of you often.
Of your power to transform, Yael, I conjure up daily.

I dress in Aramaic and press lapis into my skin.
I toil with my hands; my nails are all broken.
I cajole the stones to arrange themselves.
Singing in Ivrit, the Negev hears of your names
And willing begins its work.

We are building a road through the Negev.
I am using flint and stacking scoria.
The beetles roll the small rocks into place,
Between their horns, the ibex carries the heavy stones.
Unaided, ancient dolomite rolls up from the Arava.

They come at their own bidding,
Drawn to the call for which they have waited,
To the call that I sing loudly in the Negev,
"We are going to our mothers,
To sit at their side and learn their songs."

Ancient stones can recall the mothers' touch,
The sharpest flint remembers the matriarchs' hands
Using it to build fire and shelter,
Create food and sometimes death.
Adorned with snail shells, sparkling with salt,
Our road will take us back to our mothers,
To hear their stories and record their words.

I will not be alone, others will come,
And in unison, we will say,
"Speak to us, mothers, we know you have been waiting.
Tell us of your tents and of your travels in the Negev,
Of the time when the Jewish kings ruled,
And of your ascents to Yerushalayim.

A. E. Hayoun

Tell us again how you will return
In the likeness of the women who wander the Negev
Of the Jewish women who tend this land."

Dear mothers, I have found Dina,
She was not buried at Arbel.
Dina has been walking beside me
Wearing amaranth, she is burnished and jovial.

Robed in dew, clad in pottery,
Trailing gold and desert truffles,
Back and forth I will carry,
Words and meaning, record and voice
As I make tracks on the great Negev road.

Mothers, your road is built, the stones are set in place.
Now they need only come, the others, the women,
Out into the desert, to walk our road
And to meet you where you wait, ha'imahot, our mothers.

SHALOM

From whence is this feeling of soft, hesitant peace?
It floats in the air, and like palm fronds,
It fans cool winds into the Negev.

Winds blow up from the South,
Sand and dust hiss through my hair and teeth,
And I find myself resting in the hot midday sun.

A traveler of land and time,
I touch the ancient and walk old lands anew.
Standing heavily on this Earth,
I am both experience and word.

The source of this peace remains unknown,
And I have stopped searching for it.
Instead, I seek out joy under the sun
And take flight in the wind
On the wings of tzufit.

A. E. Hayoun

NOF

Friend, I have brought you a view,
Not just for admiring,
But a view for loving and tending.

This task is not simple, it will consume much of our time,
But such is love; it is not of rest
But of constant care and loving vigilance.

Will you join me in this task?
Expediate your answer, send it by carrier camel,
That we may begin as soon as possible.

There is no time left, and none to waste,
In protecting this land and its precious view.
There are those who pillage and use it, abuse it,
And then leave it covered with their trash
And permanently wrecked by their machines.

It is possible they do not know,
Or perhaps do not understand,
The importance of views in all the lands.
So let us show them what our care can do.
Let us love one another, ourselves, and this view.

RETURN

Desert, unchangeable as you are ancient,
But every word I speak to you
Shows in an abundance
Of new growth and beauty revealed.

I whisper to your rocks and laugh with your trees.
While I eat your fruits and play with your camels,
I remind them that it's coming.

The day will come when you will shine,
Your salt sea will be full again
And reach the balcony of Herod's palace.
The bears will come back
And the hunted eagles will fill the sky.

The women will return to the forest
To bathe in golden light.
They will climb your mountains
And wander your wadis,
All the while looking for secrets
And finding themselves.

Your magic will be revealed
And you will be cherished by your people.
All the ancient will be left unchanged,
The Negev will be renewed as of old.

A. E. Hayoun

STAR

Gazing from star to star,
I don't see them for what they are
But for the stardust they will become.

In the smooth skin of the grape,
I do crave its immediate flavor.
I wait patiently for the wine it will become.

Holding an abundance of biblical olives,
I do not see only their green freshness,
I see the rich oil they will become.

In Timna's ruddy stones of cinnabar and ore,
I see bloodshed and copper.
In the simple desert sand of the Negev,
I see its history, and a forty-year journey.

As I walk under the sun,
I am burnished into a fine light.
In the heat of the desert,
I become stardust and wine,
Oil and blood.

UNIVERSE

There is a letter that waits in another universe.
A letter that awaits our arrival to another time.
It is the letters to which all mistakes are connected,
A letter whose sound will bring with it the answers,
As it kisses the head of time and washes the feet of sound.

This mysterious sound, this unknown letter,
The four-pronged Shin, the silent sister of Aleph,
Hangs suspended between this world and the next.
The mysterious letter meets the souls coming and going,
The arriving babies and the departing elders.
Enclosed in this secret letter are the answers to the questions
That have been asked since the beginning of our time.

And when time will ring out the sound of its end,
The letter that awaits will give us the answer,
And illuminate the mystery of Israel and the Jews.
The duality of Israel both ancient and modern,
Loved and hated, existent and awaiting Mashiach
Will be revealed in one understanding.

For now, we wait to know life
In the universe of the next world.
In the shadow of its silence,
We await the unheard sound of the unknown letter.

A. E. Hayoun

HAMSIN

When the sun will return
To where it hung in the sky
At the time of its creation,
I will stride into the desert,
Legs shaking with dance,
And my arms full of perfect sunlight.

Praise and blessing will pour from my mouth,
Juice of melted fruit will dribble down my chin.
I will be spinning under the sun,
Sweat flying out from my limbs,
Dancing in the hamsin.

Human and beast will gather together
And bless the Creator His gift of the sun.
The broken glass scattered in the desert
Will return in glitter the sunlight it happily captures.

Visions in my mind will become illuminated
By the sun outside my eyelids
As only my eyes will be closed against the flying sand.
Grains of sand will be crushed
By the exposed bones of my mouth as they form a smile.

In twenty-eight years, I will meet a changed sun,
And see the light as it was at creation.
There I will remain in the sun where I shine,
Browned in the sand-filtered sunlight,
Gazing unblinkingly into a future
Untouched by the light of today.

SHIPS

Sometimes I see them,
While traveling south into the Arava.
Camels in the desert,
Standing on towering dunes
Hovering at a cliff's edge.

They are not the camels I knew,
These ships of the desert are free
Walking with out shackles.

Unfazed by the heat,
Unafraid of the cliff's edge,
These camels stand proud
In their desert home.

I am certain they carry a message for me,
A message that will make sense
Of all that has transpired.

But as I approach them,
The camels disappear
Leaving me alone in the desert,
Alone with my reason, with my answer,
For why I have come.

As I turn back,
Striding homewards,
I too begin to fade away
Like a mirage in the sunlight.

A. E. Hayoun

MEVUREHET

May your goings be in peace.
May all your ways be open.
May you receive your portion,
And find your return to your gates.

May you journey in your destiny,
And therein find love.
May peace surround you,
Peace within all your realms.

Because all the good still lies before you.

May your dreams be revealed,
All truth be made clear.
May you be cleansed of every worry,
And walk safely in your ways.

May your two hands be blessed
Be blessed to toil and create.
May the sparkle in your eyes
Forever sparkle towards mine.

Because all the good still lies before you.

A Shir of Shirim

א In the shadow of Anim, you spread a banquet for me; I bask in the biblical sun and the light of your love. Wine meets my lips and I drink deeply of your devotion.

ב Your mother's children look like their father, Dodi, but you look like their king. Your hands are strength, and your mind is justice. Rule in my kingdom, my gates are open.

ג You are scented with malkat halila, your essence is the cool night air, I am drawn to you like a moth to the moon.

ד Let me kiss your wine-stained mouth, Beloved, your flavor is richer than wine from Yatir, your eyes are like two grapes from fertile ground.

ה Beloved, I'm stippled and creased like the deserts we love so well. But you rejoice in my age; I am beautiful in the light!

ו Lover, you see behind my veils, beyond my adornments, my skin and my flesh, my soul and my truth. Come play in the field, and I will remove the last veil.

ז Your prayers are like honey, sweet and sustaining, Beloved, heard by HaShem in your sincerity and truth.

ח Lover, our children become like you with each passing day; you make them into warriors and tzadikim

ט I love you, Friend, more than my own waters. When they run out of me, through you they are replenished.

י Trust me, Beloved, with your heart and your home. By day we are like trees in Lahav, by night you enter my caves.

יא On our heads, Dodi, you pronounce chochma, binah, and daat; into our hearts you impress respect.

יב My breasts, Beloved, have fallen further with each gift of my womb, but their softness gathers you in and strips your hardship.

יג A rope cannot be pushed; pull, Lover, that I will be drawn upwards to you like the slaking water from the wells of Be'er Sheva. On your lips, you will know my powers to rejuvenate.

יד I am endangered, Dodi, so you protect me; I am the southern red flower, and you safeguard my growth. You are the shade in the forest under which I bloom.

A. E. Hayoun

ש Named for a king, warrior, and poet, Beloved, you are blessed with your namesake!

ש In our forest of fruit trees, you remove the weeds that threaten their growth and I pour abundant water on their roots.

י The last veil has fallen, down at my feet; my breasts stand between us. My heart beats like the wings of the tzufit; I delight in your laughter.

יי Friend, you are wonderous, when I search for blossoms to adorn my hair, you bring me za'atar for my garden and rakefet for my hair.

ט׳ Go out to the forest, Lover, bring me kalaniot. While my womb bleeds, I gaze at them and yearn for you. Then I wash myself in life and join you again

כ In your presence, Beloved, I am the levia resting in the shade. But tell me, Lover, in your absence where shall I rest? I pace like the levia in the fields, waiting to hear your roar.

כא Your shoulders bear sunspots, I eat them by night. I wake in the morning and my eyes are alight.

כב The corners of our house are rounded like columns, our sons are like oaks, our daughters like date palms, you have infused them with your strength, Dodi.

כג I walked around you in circles, Beloved. I will encircle you for all the days of my life.

כד Your head shape is pleasing, curved, and strong, Lover, it carries your curls dark and biblical. It is the head embossed on the currency of my heart.

כה Oils golden and fragrant glisten on my limbs, between my breasts, a snake slithers; through my hair, a comb of fingers.

כו I am the camel in the forest, enjoying the sun in the valley. Meet me, Beloved, where I choose to rest.

כז Arise to your place, O king of my house, bless us our wine, and speak to the angels.

כח Your nose is noble, distinctive, and familiar, it is the nose of your ancestors, that of Hayoun. The Hayouns exiled West, have returned to their desert, and by their river they find their rest.

כט When you wash yourself, my own hands despair, they are drawn to you, My Love, like the caracal to the waters of Ein Gedi.

The Camel in the Forest

ל You are a biblical oak, Dodi, you are timeless. Your shade gives respite to the weak and your roots run deep.

לא The Omer you count and we wait for Shavuot, to celebrate together, Beloved, the giving of our Life.

לב Beloved, the gold you bring me warms my skin by day until you return to warm me by night. The gold I buy for myself possesses no such quality.

לג In the shade of the eucalyptus, I find my beloved. I find him in my hands awake with love.

לד I am burnished, sometimes tarnished, Beloved, but you speak to me as though I am fine gold.

לה Like lipid salt pools are your words, Dodi, I float in your eternal wisdom. I am a salt pillar, steadfast in my love.

לו At sunrise I wake to sing and extol, Friend, by night you pray and secure our walls.

לז You sit at my table, a king at a banquet, our children's laughter covers our table in malachite and gold. Our joys are many, but our children are our crown.

לח Like the iris of Tel Arad, I blossom in the desert, like the brown curves of its petals my body browns in the Negev sun. My curves are fed by fruits of the land.

לט My skin is cracked like upended earth, but you, Lover, see my mind. We converse in a language honed by the years, a language all our own.

מ Between forests, Beloved, you built me a home. My children I bring forth under its roof, you are the foundation supporting the sands.

מא Plant a vineyard and I will tend it; plant your seed and I will nurture it. Beloved, we have gardened together, our children are our harvest of love.

מב I am woman, I am earth. My caves you have explored, the one beyond my eyes, the two behind my knees, Beloved, the one between my legs.

מג We are fruit trees in the wild garden, we bring forth fragrance and fruit. Our union is a delight to those around us.

מד Behold, our many flaws, Beloved, may we spend our whole lives transforming them. We are mortals in love.

מה I made a bed of wild grasses; you sustained us with the wine of Yatir; the moon provided the light by which I delighted in your face.

מו My beloved is my friend and I am his, into our souls we gaze with our eyes wide open.

מז Like a sacred view I wish to gaze at you until your sun has set; your horizons are full of wonder.

מח His left hand under my neck, his right hand drawing me towards him. Willingly, Beloved, I come willingly.

מט Speak to me, Lover, words only true, make me your equal. I speak to you candidly, there are no traps laid in our love.

נ Like a rose without water, my color is vibrant but my petals begin to wilt. Water me, tend me, Beloved, embrace my thorns.

נא I thrill at the sight of my beloved returning from the fields. Like a tree in a deep valley, Dodi, you overwhelm me.

נב In the month of Moznaim, the days grow shorter, but upon your arrival, the world became more expansive.

נג When you brought me into our home, you knew love would follow, Beloved. Together we've built our love and the home no longer matters.

נד Like a river in the desert, I give of myself until I am parched and then my beloved says, "Rest." He enters my riverbed and my springs come alive.

נה We were here before, Beloved, Hayouns in the desert. Our children are the river and our family enlivens.

נו I adjure the jackals by night and the feral cats by day, do not eat the songbirds nor devour their eggs. To birdsong do my beloved and I rejoice in our love.

נז By moonlight you wake me, Lover, eating my breasts like fruit; they sustain you through the night until my arms embrace you in the morning.

נח Like the pashosh, Beloved, I flit around your garden, eating your fruits and nesting in your leaves.

נט My heart knows the distance, Lover, between yours to mine. With my ear to the ground, I hear our love thrum.

ס The passionfruit vines have sent out their tendrils, so too my fingers wrap around your columns. Dodi, like the grapevine, I tendril your towers.

The Camel in the Forest

אט My beloved is like the rains in Nissan, respected and praised, needed and adored.

בט Seize my hair and pull me downward; Lover, lay me by the carob tree, under its familiar scent.

גט Winter has passed, Beloved, and spring is in the desert. The people are singing, but we have been singing together through each season.

דט Lover, I eat your fingers, they are like wild fennel; your scent is like rich earth and sunburnt eucalyptus, stay near me.

הט Bring me the earthworms, bring them to my garden, Beloved, that it will bear abundant fruit.

וט In our garden, the pears are still green but the shesek are ripe, Lover, we are not always in season.

זט Like an ancient dovecote are you, Dodi, you have apertures of love for all who need you.

חט On this spinning Earth, we have found our axis. When you are the sun, I am the moon.

טט My lover is mine and I am his friend, together our robes leave trails through the garden.

ע Let me bathe you under the stars, then lay me down upon the ground, pull the thistles from my hair, and, Beloved, I will sing songs to your soul.

אע Graveyard neighbor and celestial friend; we are bashert mishamayim. Our bones will break free of their linens to find each other, and between stars, our souls will meet again.

בע Like water from a well, I pull you into me, you cleanse me and refresh me in all your neutrality.

גע Beloved, your teeth are like pillars, strong and polished, a glimpse of them in your smile and my soul sings out.

דע As we live on our land, our inheritance, our gift, so too my heart lives assuredly in your love.

הע Like a mountain in the Salt Sea am I to your hill in the desert. Dodi, we have reached great heights.

וע Capture the tzufit, Beloved, for only a moment. Show me his wings and iridescent feathers. Release him into our garden that he may call to his beloved.

זע Lover, my ears listen for your voice in the sounds of the earth, your voice is the sound of my breath and my heart.

A. E. Hayoun

עז Like a bee, My Love, you fly to my nectar and drink, my blossom swells and all my petals quiver.

עט Between the moonset and moonrise, I dwell on you, Beloved, as I dwell under starlight.

פ In our bed, my limbs seek you out, Friend, like tree roots seek groundwater. In your fragrant boughs, I dream of the desert.

פא You walk through the shuk, Beloved, pressing, smelling, and tasting the fruits. Walking beside you, my body is jealous.

פב My hand on your head, my hand on your shoulder; you breathe deeply my scent of morning orange blossoms and eternal peace.

פג Like a camel, Dodi, your eyelashes curl; protecting your eyes and taunting my soul.

פד Upon waking, Beloved, I gather the linens. I wash them, dry them, smooth them, and scent them; at night I will love you upon sandalwood and flax.

פה In Sinai, I see you, burnished in the sun, laying in the waters of Sharm el-Sheikh. Beloved, the ocean is made sweeter.

פו In my hands are apricots and figs, on my stomach is amaranth, and my legs are wrapped in grape leaves; I am a feast, Beloved, to nourish and delight.

פז Like lentils and gold are your eyes at sunset, Lover, by night they are windows through which I see your thoughts.

פח The explosions of the sun are the magnitude of my love; they reverberate from my heart to yours. When I see you, solar light fills my stomach.

פט Like shirat hadekel your voice washes over me; drowning out the noises of desert and night.

צ Saffron and turmeric stain my hands, Dodi, your skin is orange and yellow. Red threads streak my hair, find me in the saffron fields.

צא Hidden by palms, caressed by the wind, my beloved and I press into the earth. We leave behind another desert crater.

צב We are an essence, Lover, delicious in scent, bitter in flavor. Soft like rose petals, untouchable like nettle.

צג My toes are like capers, my legs like squills; I am of this land, Beloved, you forage within me.

The Camel in the Forest

עָר Like barley in the summer heat is my hair; in the winter it is long on the pillow beside you. By morning all of me is curled and softly crushed.

עָה Your words are like camun, fragrant and strong; my hands touch your curls, my mouth drinks your wine.

עִו You are truffle in the desert, I am rockrose in the sand. Your surety in me increases your value.

עִז You bring me hilba and ezov, I prepare za'atar and zchoug. You provide and I prepare, Lover. We are a match for each other.

עָח I am myself in myriads and you know them all, our thoughts intertwine. Friend, you are well met.

עָט My legs, Beloved, they part like Yam Suf, only you lay in my seabed and float in currents. You are the moon, magnetizing my tides.

ק On Har Hiran I stand and call to you, from Har Hevron you answer and the Negev blooms. Between you and me is the camel in the forest.

GLOSSARY OF FOREIGN WORDS AND PHRASES

Abba – Hebrew, father
Adam – Hebrew, first man, husband of Hava (Eve)
Adom – Hebrew, red
Ahashverosh – Hebrew from Old Persian, king of Persia (Hebrew year 3392), husband of Queen Esther.
al alekum salaam – Arabic, "and peace upon you" is the traditional reply after being greeted by someone with "Salaam alekum."
al-Aqsa – Arabic, lit. "the furthest mosque," refers to the Islamic mosque compound built on top of the Jewish Temple Mount. Also refers to the silver-domed mosque building within the compound built in seventh century.
al-Arabiya Diyalna – Arabic, a term for the spoken Arabic of Moroccan Jews.
al-Farhud – Arabic, pogrom. The violent pogrom conducted by Muslims against the Jewish population in Baghdad, Iraq in June 1941 2,500 Jewish families suffered injury, rape, and loss of property. Approximately 180 Jews were murdered and buried in a mass grave.
al-Furat – Arabic, the Euphrates River that flows through Türkiye, Syria, and Iraq.
Allah – Arabic, God
al-Maqdis – Arabic, refers to bayt al-maqdis which is the Arabic equivalent of the Hebrew Beit HaMikdash, the Jewish holy temple. This is the name in Arabic used by Muslims for the holy city of Jerusalem. The modern political Palestinian movement often incorrectly associated this term with Masjid al-Aqsa that was built on top of the ruins of the Jewish holy temple (Beit HaMikdash), but not only was the al-Aqsa built several thousand years after the Jewish Holy Temple, the name Masjid al-Aqsa translate to "the farthest mosque" implying the furthest from Islam's holy site of Mecca in Saudi Arabia.
al-Maqdisi – Arabic, the term for an Arab person who lives in Jerusalem, a Jerusalemite.
al-Masjid An-Nabawi – Arabic, The Prophet's Mosque. First mosque built by Muhammad in Medina. Second holiest site in Islam.
al-Nakba – Arabic, lit. catastrophe, is a day memorializing the deaths of Arabs who fled or fell fighting in the Israel War of Independence in 1948. Commemorated annually on May 15th, it is often incorrectly referred to as a memorial day for the "ethnic cleansing of Palestinians" during the Israel War of Independence in 1948. This is factually incorrect because the Palestinian people in 1948 were Jews living in the British Mandate Palestine, the Arabs living there were referred to as Arabs and came from surrounding Arab countries. There was no ethnic cleansing of any type of Arab in 1948 because most Arabs remained in 1948 State of Israel throughout the war or returned shortly after the war. These Arabs were

the grandparents of the two million Arabs that live as first-class citizens in Israel today. It is important to note that the Israel War of Independence occurred because the Arab population in British Mandate Palestine declined the option of Arab statehood and subsequently local Arabs and the armies from five Arab countries launched an immediate attack on the Jews in the newly formed state of Israel.

am hofshi b'artzenu – Hebrew, "a people free in our land" is a stanza from the 19th century poem HaTikva written by Naphtali Herz Imber.

Am Yisrael chai – Hebrew, lit. "the people of Israel live."

Amba - Hebrew, etymologically derived from the Sanskrit word Amra meaning mango. Amba is a tangy mango condiment of Baghdadi Jewish origin brought to Israel from India with the Baghdadi Jews who returned from exile in the diaspora.

Ani beseder, mami, hakol beseder – Hebrew, "I am okay, dear, everything is fine."

Anim (synagogue) – Hebrew, Anim is a Byzantine era synagogue and Jewish village located South of Hevron in the Yatir forest. It was built in the fourth century and turned into a mosque during the Arab occupation in the 8th century. Anim is mentioned in the Tanakh (Hebrew Bible) in Joshua 15:50.

Apartheid – Afrikaans, apartness. The term was coined in 1940s South Africa to describe the system of institutionalized racial segregation between "Black" and "White" people in South Africa and Namibia until the 1990s. This term is incorrectly used in reference to Israel where people claim Israel is an apartheid state in which Arabs do not have equal rights. This is false and the proof is in the Arab Israeli parliament members, equal voting rights, and equal opportunities for Arabs and minorities throughout Israel to mention just a few freedoms Arabs in Israel enjoy as equal citizens.

Arab – Arabic, a type of semitic people indigenous to the Arabian Peninsula, now inhabiting most of the middle east and north Africa.

Arad (fortress) – Hebrew, a bronze age stronghold on a hill in the Negev desert, west of the Dead Sea. It is mentioned multiple times in the Tanakh (Hebrew Bible) in the books Deuteronomy, Numbers, and Judges.

Arak – Arabic, lit. sweat. Arak is a Levantine alcohol made from anise seed and grapes.

Arava – Hebrew, wilderness. The geographic region of desert south of the Dead Sea basin in Israel along the border with Jordan.

Arbel (mountain) – Hebrew, located in the Lower Galilee region near Tveria (Tiberius), Mt. Arbel is known for its high cliffs, ancient cave-fortress, ancient synagogue ruins, and the burial place of Dinah only daughter of Yaakov and Leah.

Aretz Yisrael – Hebrew, Land of Israel. One of the terms used for biblical Israel and the modern state of Israel.

Arka – Hebrew, one of the seven earths mentioned in The Legend of the Jews and the book of the Zohar. Tevel is the fifth highest Earth, the one we inhabit. The Zohar first teaches that these seven earths are arranged like an onion in subsequent layers downwards into the Earth, but a second source in the Zohar teaches that these seven earths are actually the seven continents on our Earth each with its own climate and geography as well as different looking people, language, and cultures.

Ashkelon – Hebrew, modern city in Israel along the Mediterranean coast, north of Gaza, and south of Tel Aviv.

Ashkenazim – Hebrew, etymological roots from the biblical name for Japhet's son. Originally a term for Jews who lived in exile in Germany and France but has since been expanded to include Jews who lived in exile throughout Central and Eastern Europe.

Avatiah - Hebrew, watermelon

Anavim - Hebrew, grapes

Avdat – Hebrew name derived from the name of Nabataean King Obodas I. Avdat is an ancient Nabataean city and fortress located in the Negev desert south of Sde Boker. The fortress was built on a hilltop above the river Tzin watercourse in the Hellenistic period. It was a major station along the Incense Route.

Avinu – Hebrew, our father. A term used to refer to several of the Jewish patriarchs (Avraham, Yitzhak, and Yaakov). Avinu is also used to refer to Gd (HaKadosh Baruchu), our father.

Avraham/Abraham/Ibrahim – Hebrew, the first patriarch of the Jewish people, husband of Sara (Sarah), father of Ishmael and Yitzhak.

Avud – Hebrew, lost

Aza (Gaza) – Hebrew from Aramaic, lit. "the strong." Aza is another name for Gaza, an ancient Philistine city along the southwest coast of the Mediterranean in ancient Israel. Aza is the modern Hebrew way to pronounce the name for the Gaza Strip.

Babka - Yiddish, a sweet, twisted chocolate braided bread that originated in the Jewish communities of Poland and Eastern Europe. It is a popular pastry in Israel and in the Jewish diaspora.

Baharat – Arabic from Persian, lit. spices. Baharat is a common Levantine spice mixture in which diverse cultures and regions include different spices like allspice, cloves, cumin, black pepper, turmeric, saffron, and many more.

Balagan - Hebrew, mess

Bardelas - Hebrew, leopard

Bashert bashamayim – Yiddish and Hebrew, a phrase loosely translates to "a match made in heaven" based on the Talmudic teaching that tells us that forty days before a fetus is formed, a heavenly echo declares whom it is intended to marry.

Bayit -Hebrew, house

Be'er LaHai-Roi – Hebrew, lit. "well of the Living One seeing me," a biblical well located west of Kadesh in the Negev desert.

Be'er Sheva – Hebrew, lit. "well of seven," a city of wells located in the Negev desert south of Hevron purchased by Avraham and established as a city. A major Negev city in modern day southern Israel.
Bedouin – Arabic, nomadic, pastoral Arab tribes that have historically inhabited desert regions through the Arabian Peninsula, North Africa, the Levant, and Mesopotamia.
Beit Knesset – Hebrew, synagogue or shul, a place of worship for Jews, where Jews attend weekly Torah readings, ritual holy day ceremonies, and other ethno-religious services.
Beit Lechem (Bethlehem) – Hebrew, lit. "House of Bread." An ancient biblical town located in ancient Judea, south of Jerusalem. Known as the birthplace of Yeshu (Jesus). Modern day Beit Lechem is located in the "West Bank." Prior to the Oslo Accords, Beit Lechem population was 60% Christian. Under the governance of the Palestinian Authority, the Christian population has decreased to less than 20%.
Beit Mikdash/Beit HaMikdash – Hebrew, "holy temple" or "The Holy Temple" of the Jewish people in Jerusalem. The ruins of the Jewish temple in Jerusalem are located on the modern-day Temple Mount in the Old City of Jerusalem. Most of the ruins, aside from the remaining exterior wall which forms the Kotel (Wailing Wall) were destroyed during both the Roman and subsequent Muslim occupations. The al-Aqsa compound is built on the ruins of the Jewish Holy Temple. The Arabic word for Jerusalem "al-Quds" comes from the Hebrew words Kodesh and Mikdash both come from the Hebrew root word "holy" in reference to the holy Jewish temple and the holy city of Jerusalem.
Beitza - Hebrew, egg
Belshazzar – Old Persian, King of Persia (Babylon) who ascended the throne of Persia in 374 BCE. After the takeover and exile of the Jewish kingdoms, Belshazzar desecrated the sacred vessels of the Jewish holy temple at his feast. A hand appeared and wrote a mysterious sentence on the wall, a sentence that defied all interpretation until captive Judean Daniel was brought from captivity to interpret its meaning. The sentence prophesied the demise of Belshazzar and the dissolution of his kingdom. King Darius succeeded Belshazzar. Belshazzar is written about in the book of Daniel in the Tanakh (Hebrew bible).
Bereshit sheli - Hebrew, "my genesis"
Bezrat HaShem – Hebrew, G-d willing, lit. "with Gd's help."
Bima – Hebrew, a raised platform in a synagogue on which the Torah scroll is placed and read.
Bourekas -Hebrew, a Levantine and southern European flaky, filo pastry traditional filled with cheese, potatoes, or mushrooms. Most popular within Sephardic Jewish communities.
British Mandate/British Mandate of Palestine – see Palestine
Bubbe/s - Yiddish, grandmother/s
Bulgarit - Hebrew, lit. Bulgarian, is a salty Bulgarian-style feta cheese.
Cafe - Hebrew, coffee

Cafe au lait - French, latte coffee or milk coffee
Cafe Shahor - Hebrew, an unfiltered finely ground Turkish-style coffee traditionally prepared in a Finjan (long-handled coffeepot).
Cafe ve'ma'afe - Hebrew, "coffee and pastry"
Calev (Caleb) – Hebrew, biblical leader of the tribe of Yehuda (Judah). Calev married Miriam, the sister of Moshe (Moses) and Aharon; as well as Batya, the princess of Egypt who drew Moshe from the Nile. He had children with both women who became leaders of the Jews while the sojourned in the desert after their exodus from slavery in Egypt.
Caracal – Spanish from Turkish, a medium-sized wild cat native to Africa, the Middle East, and Central Asia.
Challah - Hebrew, a traditional Jewish braided bread typically eaten ceremonially on Shabbat and Jewish holy days.
Chochma, bina, and daat – Chochma (wisdom/concept), bina (understanding/comprehension), and daat (knowledge/depth) are three words that represent the three interconnected processes of receiving a spark of insight/idea and transforming it from its initial idea to a fully developed and applied concept. The words chochma, bina, and daat as standalone words in Hebrew are desirous qualities that all Jews are encouraged to seek out and bestow upon their children.
Choled – Hebrew, mole
Chralme – Hebrew from Arabic, a traditional North African tomato sauce and fish stew popular among Libyan and Moroccan Jewish communities.
Couscous – Arabic from Amazigh origin, a traditional North African dish of steamed granules of rolled semolina. Traditionally served with a vegetable stew and meatballs or roasted meat on top.
Cusbara – Hebrew, cilantro. Refers to both the leafy cilantro herb as well as coriander (cilantro) seeds.
Cyrus the Great – Old Persian, founder of the Achaemenid Empire, one of the earliest known Persian empires. Cyrus ruled from 559 to 530 BCE and is credited with his tolerant view of the exile Jews within his kingdom and allowing them to return to the land of Israel and rebuild the Temple.
Dafna - Hebrew, laurel, bay leaf, a leaf from the laurel tree used in cooking as a seasoning, historically used in a crown placed on the head of victors in ancient Greece.
Darius I – King Darius I of Persia conquered Babylon IN 372 BCE, beginning the second exile of the Jewish people. He was favorably inclined toward the Jews, appointed Daniel the prophet as chief minister of the realm and ruled for only one year before dying. Was succeeded by Cyrus the Great.
Darius II – Son of Perian King Ahashverosh and Queen Esther. Succeeded the throne in 355 BCE. The second temple was completed under his rule in 349 BCE.

Darom (Dar-Rom) - Hebrew, south. Unclear etymological Hebrew source, thought to come from the words "dar" which means "to live" or "situated" and "rom" which could mean "high up" in reference to the higher position of the sun in the Negev desert.

Darom Adom – Red South, annual anemone flower festival in the Negev

David (King) – Born in Beit Lechem (Bethlehem) to Yeshi and Netzevet. Anointed king of Israel in 877 BCE. Married to Michal, Avigail, and Batsheva. Compiled the book of Tehillim (Psalms). Succeeded by King Shlomo (Solomon).

Dayenu – Hebrew, lit. "enough for us," a phrase traditionally declared during the Jewish holy day of Pesach (Passover).

Dekel – Hebrew, palm tree

Delek - Hebrew, gas/petrol

Dhimmi – Arabic, Arabic, term for a non-Muslim living in a Muslim state or under Muslim conquest. Though dhimmi translates to "protected" in Arabic, the status of dhimmis in Muslim society was that of second-class citizens who were often humiliated for being non-Muslim and were taxed a "special" dhimmi tax.

Dijlah – Arabic, Tigris River in ancient Persia/modern-day Iraq

Dina – Hebrew, the firstborn daughter of Yaakov and Leah. Said to be buried at Mt. Arbel near Kineret (the Sea of Galilee).

Dodi – Hebrew, a term of love or endearment roughly translated as "gift" or "beloved".

Druze/Druzi – An ethnoreligious minority group of Arabs in Israel. Though they are not Muslims their ethnoreligion is based in Shia Islam. Their belief system is based in monotheism and is an Abrahamic faith in which they revere as prophets many people including Abraham, Moses, Jethro, Muhammad, and Jesus to name a few. The Druze people are loyal Israeli citizens who serve in the military and high governmental positions.

Dukhifat – Hebrew, the migratory hoopoe bird (Upupidae). Israel's national bird.

Dunam – Hebrew from Turkish, a measure of land area, the equivalent of 900 square meters.

Edom – Hebrew, a mountainous region of land between southern Jordan and the Negev Desert in Israel.

Ein Gedi – Hebrew, Ein Gedi means "spring of the kid (young male goat)" and is an oasis, an archeological site, and a nature reserve in Israel on the west side of the Dead Sea near Masada. Kibbutz Ein Gedi was established nearby in 1954.

Emigrees - French, a person who emigrates from one country to another

Ephron HaHiti – Hebrew, son of Zohar, a Hittite. Landowner who sold the cave of the Machpela to Avraham.

Eshkolit/ot - Hebrew, grapefruit/grapefruits

Eshtamoa – Hebrew, 4th century ancient Jewish synagogue located in the Judean hills south of Hevron. The name of a river of the same name flows through the Yati region.
Esther – Old Persian, means "shining star." First cousin of Mordecai, selected as King Ahasuerus's queen in the 4th century BCE after his wife Vashti's execution. At Mordecai's behest, she brought about Ahasuerus's annulment of evil Haman's decree calling for the extermination of the Jews.
Evanim – Hebrew, stones
Ezov – Hebrew, hyssop
Falafel – Hebrew, a traditional Levantine deep-fried ball-shaped fritter made from broad beans and/or chickpeas.
Finjan – Turkish, long-handled coffee pot.
From the River to the Sea – English from Arabic, a poor translation of the Arabic slogans "From water to water, Palestine will be Arab" and "From the river to the sea, Palestine will be Arab." The Arabic slogans are transliterated as "min al-mayyeh lil-mayyeh Filastin 'arabiyyeh" and "min al-nahr ila al-bahr Filastin 'arabiyyeh" respectively. This slogan in both of its variation is calling for the destruction of the state and land of Israel and the ethnic cleansing of the Jewish people as well as any other non-Arab (Muslim) minority groups in that region. This slogan perpetuates the prevalent Muslim belief that Islam should be spread throughout the world and any country, religion, or people group that stands in the way of Arab, Muslim colonization should be destroyed.
Gabriel/Gavriel/Jabreel – English/Hebrew/Arabic, biblical angel portrayed as a messenger in Judaism. Later Christian and Islamic texts portray Gabriel/Jabreel as a messenger between Gd and humans.
Galut – Hebrew, exile
Gamal Shlomo – Hebrew, lit. "Solomon's camel," praying mantis
Gamal/Gmalim – Hebrew, camel/camels
Gan Eden – Hebrew, Garden of Eden
Gateway to the Negev - a range of small hills in the Lahav forest between the Shfela region and the Negev desert that Highway 6 cuts through.
G-d/Gd – abbreviated out of respect for the holy name of Gd.
Geniza – Hebrew, hiding/storage. A repository or storage area within a Jewish community where any sacred text or fragment containing the name of Gd is considered holy and is collected and stored in the geniza until it can be ritually buried, ensuring respectful disposal of sacred items.
Geula – Hebrew, redemption
Giva/Givat/Gvaot – Hebrew, hill/Hill/hills
Golah – Hebrew, diaspora
Golan - Hebrew, a region in the north of Israel along the Syrian and Lebanese border, a mountain plateau region primarily known as the Golan Heights.

Golem – Hebrew, chrysalis. Yiddish, a creature from Jewish folklore made from clay and can be brought to life by a learned sage or rabbi who knows the proper mystical use of the Hebrew alphabet. According to legend, the golem had the word "emet" (truth) inscribed on its forehead after which it would do the rabbis bidding. If the first Hebrew letter of the word "emet," the Aleph, was removed then the golem would be "deactivated." The golem was tasked with serving its creator and protecting the Jewish community from harm.
Guiava - Hebrew, guava
Gush Katif – Hebrew, following the Six-Day War in 1967 (a war begun with the mobilization of Syrian, Lebanese, Iragi, Egyptian, and Jordanian troops towards Israeli borders) Israeli towns were built in the Gaza Strip over subsequent decades. The area was known for its greenhouse agriculture and flower production. When the Israeli government decided to unilaterally disengage from the Gaza Strip in 2005 in hopes that the Arabs in the Gaza Strip would use the land to create their own prosperous country under a sustainable independent government. In 2005, Israelis were forcibly removed from Gush Katif, synagogues with dismantled by the Israeli military, and Jewish graves where exhumed from the Gaza Strip leaving nothing Israeli or Jewish behind that could be desecrated by the Arabs in the Gaza Strip. Since gaining independence in 2005, the Arabs in the Gaza Strip were governed by Fatah until 2007 when Hamas staged a bloody coup overthrowing the Fatah government. Despite massive amounts of monetary and physical humanitarian aid from Israel and countries around the world, the Gaza Strip has been and remains a hot bed of terrorism and violence despite every opportunity afforded Hamas and Gazans to build a sustainable future for their citizens.
Gvulot – Hebrew, borders
Hadaf - Hebrew, mole
Hadra – Arabic, "presence"
Hagar/Hajar – Hebrew/Arabic, the matriarch Sara's handmaiden, consort to Avraham, mother of Ishmael. The Jewish midrash teaches that Hagar was actually an Egyptian princess sent home with Sara and Avraham after their sojourn in Egypt. The Sages also teach that Hagar is the same as Keturah, Avraham's second wife.
HaLevana - Hebrew, lit. "The White One," a name for the moon.
Halva – Hebrew from Persian, a sweet Levantine confectionery made with flour, oil, tahini, and added flavors.
Haman – Old Persian, the advisor to the Persian king Ahashverosh, who plotted to annihilate the Jewish people, but his plan was thwarted by Queen Esther's presence within the Persian palace and her fasting and prayer.
Hamas – Arabic, is an acronym for Harakat al-Muqawama al-Islamiya which means "Islamic Resistance Movement." Hamas is a recognized terrorist organization of Arab Sunni Islamist and is the ruling government in the Gaza Strip since 2007.

Hami – Hebrew, lit. my father-in-law
Hamsin – Hebrew from Arabic, a term used throughout the Levant to describe the dry, hot sandstorm like winds that blow through the region seasonally.
Har - Hebrew, mountain
Har Hiran/Hiran - Hebrew, Mount Hiran, a low mountain in the Northern Negev, located near Yatir Forest.
Har Sinai – Hebrew, biblical Mount Sinai, though its exact location is unknown, most scholars agree it is in the Sinai Peninsula in modern-day Egypt. The mountain on which Moshe received the Ten Commandments from Gd.
Haram al-Sharif – Arabic, "Noble Sanctuary" is an Islamic religious site located on top of the ruins of the Jewish Temple Mount. The site encompasses al-Aqsa Mosque and the Dome of the Rock shrine. According to Islamic tradition it is the site from which Muhammad ascended to heaven.
Harisa - Hebrew, a North African spicy, aromatic red pepper condiment traditionally prepare and used in Moroccan and Tunisian cuisine and includes red chiles, garlic, olive oil, and spices
HaShem – Hebrew, lit. The Name, a respectful way to refer to Gd while avoiding directly pronouncing the name of Gd reflecting a reverence and recognition of the sanctity of Gd's name.
Hasida – Hebrew, crane bird
Hasidic – Hebrew, from the word Hasid meaning "pious." Hasidic Judaism is defined by its strict adherence to Jewish law (halakha), dedicated prayer and study, and joyous singing and dancing as an expression of praise and devotion to Gd.
HaTikva – Hebrew, "The Hope" Israel's national anthem. The lyrics are originally a poem composed by Naftali Herz Imber in the 19th century, the melody is derived from a European folk tune.
Hatzil/im - Hebrew, eggplant/s
Hava - Hebrew, first woman, Eve, wife of Adam, mother of Cayin (Cain), Havel (Abel), and Shet (Seth).
Havdalah – Hebrew, from the root word "to differentiate." A Jewish ritual ceremony performed at the end of Shabbat (see Shabbat) that marks the separation of the holy day of Shabbat from the rest of the week. Special prayers are recited and blessings are said over wine, spices, and a candle.
Hawaij - Hebrew, a Yemenite spice blend traditionally used in soup, stews, and meat preparations. The spice blend typically includes a varying mixture of cumin, lime, ginger, clove, coriander, and turmeric as well as other spices.
Hayoun – Hebrew, a Hebrew surname from the root word for "life" and "strength," sometimes translated at "enliven" or "strengthen."
Hel - Hebrew, cardamom

Herod – Greek, name of several rulers of the Judea during the Roman occupation of the land of Israel and Judea. Herod the Great was the most notable of all the Herodian rulers. Appointed during the first century BCE by the Roman Senate in 40 BCE, he ruled until his death in 4 BCE.
Hevron - Hebrew, the ancient and modern Jewish city of Hebron located in the Southern Judean mountains. Hevron is the site of the Cave of Machpelah (Cave of the Patriarchs).
Hilazon Midbari – Hebrew, lit. "desert snail. A species of white snail prevalent in the Negev Desert. Not to be confused with the biblical snail by the same named allegedly used to create the special blue dye called tekhelet used for dying tlitot.
Hilba – Hebrew, fenugreek seeds
Hira Cave – Arabic, a cave in the mountains of Jabal al-Nour, outside the city of Mecca. Allegedly, the Islamic prophet Muhammad received the verses of the Quran while meditating in the cave.
Horva/Horvat – Hebrew, ruins/Ruins
Hummus - Hebrew, a Levantine garbanzo bean dip made with lemon, olive oil, water, garlic, and spices.
Hutmit -Hebrew, hollyhocks
Hutzpa – Yiddish/Hebrew, extreme self-confidence, or audacity.
Ibrahim – Arabic, the first patriarch of the Jewish people, husband of Sara (Sarah), father of Ishmael/Ismael and Yitzhak. A prophet in Islam.
Idit/Edith – Hebrew, the name of biblical Lot's wife.
Imaot – Hebrew, mothers/matriarchs
Isaac/Yitzhak – Hebrew, son of Avraham and Sara, half-brother of Ishmael, husband to Rivka, and father to twin brothers Yaakov (Jacob) and Esav (Esau).
Ishmael/Ismail – Hebrew/Arabic, son of Avraham conceived of Hagar handmaiden to Sara. Ishmael is the patriarch of several Arab nations, but not all. Ishmael/Ismail is a prophet in Islam.
Islam – Arabic, lit. submission or surrender. Islam is the Muslim monotheistic religion as revealed through Muhammad as the self-proclaimed prophet of Allah. The religion originated in the Arabian Peninsula in the seventh century.
Ismi– Arabic, "My name is…"
Israelites – of Greek etymology. The term Israelites was used beginning in the 12th century BCE to refer to a Jewish person from the land of Israel. Commonly used in the Christian Bible to refer to Jewish people.
Ivri/Ivrim – Hebrew, singular/plural. A term for Avraham and his Jewish descendants because they alone spoke the language of Ever (Eber) the descendant of Noah who was the ancestor of Avraham. Ever also means "opposite side," relating to Avraham's belief in one Gd rather than many man-made gods as was common in the region.
Ivrit, Hebrew, the Hebrew language.
Iyar – Hebrew from Old Persian, the second and eight months in the Hebrew calendar usually coincides with the Gregorian months of April

and May. Iyar is an anacronym for "I am HaShem who heals" meaning Iyar is known as a month of healing, Iyar is also related to the Hebrew word "ohr" which means light or radiance.

Izrael – the name Israel as English-speakers hear it pronounced by Hebrew-speakers.

Jabreel – Arabic, the angel Gabriel (see Gabriel).

Jew/s – English, singular/plural. A name for the ancient people of Israel from the region of Israel and Judea. From the etymological progression of Yehuda (Hebrew) to Yehudi (Aramaic) to Ioudaios (Latin from Greek) to Juiu (Old French) and finally Jew (Middle English).

Judaism – The monotheistic ethno-religion of the Jewish people dating back 4,000 years. It is comprised of spiritual, cultural, and legal totality of beliefs and practices of the Jewish people. Jewish can practice their Judaism anywhere in the world, but Jews and Judaism are tied intrinsically, historically, and archaeologically to the land of Israel, modern day Israel, Jerusalem, and the "West Bank."

Judea/Judean – English from Hebrew, the southern region of ancient Israel, the modern-day region of Yehuda in the "West Bank." A Judean is a person from Judea, a Jewish person. Following the Roman occupation of ancient Israel and the exile of the Jewish people, the name for Judea and all the regions in Israel were changed to the Greek word Palestina, the name for the region of "south Syria" in the Levant.

Ka'ba – Arabic, cube. The Ka'ba is the holiest shrine in Islam. It is the cube-shaped building in the courtyard of the Great Mosque at Mecca and it contains a black stone that is sacred to followers of Islam.

Kalaniyot – Hebrew, anemones, a protected red flower that grows in the Negev desert in spring.

Kar - Hebrew, cold

Karkash – Hebrew, lit. intestines. Karkash is the Hebrew botanical name of the Yellow Bladder Senna plant. A yellow-flowering bush plant that grows in the Negev desert.

Kasher Badatz – a kosher certification for food or eating establishments by the kosher organization Badatz which is an acronym for "Beit Din Tzedek" which translates to "Court of Justice." Badatz oversees the ingredients, processes, and facilities used to prepare food according to kosher dietary laws.

Keffiyeh – Arabic, a traditional headdress worn by men from certain regions in the Middel East. It is a square woven scarf, usually made of cotton.

Keturah – Hebrew, "incense" or "fragrant." The second wife of Avraham whom he married after the death of Sara. The Jewish sage Rashi states that Keturah was the secret or second name of Hagar who became Avraham's second wife.

Kfar – Hebrew, rural village or small community

Khaybar – Arabic, a city in Saudia Arabia. Prior to the brutal Muslim conquest of the area in the seventh century, Khaybar was populated primarily by a Jews before the Khaybar massacre when all Jews in the region and city were either murdered or raped and driven out. The Khaybar massacre against the Jews was led by Muhammad and his army. In recent years the slogan, "Khaybar, Khaybar ya Yahud," which calls for the massacre of Jews today as they were massacred by Muhammad's army in the seventh century, has become commonplace in pro-Palestinian protests and marches.

Kikar – Hebrew, roundabout

Kippa/ot - Hebrew, singular/plural. Name for the traditional head covering worn by Jewish men.

Kishu - Hebrew, zucchini

Kitzitzot - Hebrew, meatballs

L'Chaim– Hebrew, lit. "to life," a traditional Jewish toast said before drinking alcohol under celebratory or auspicious circumstance.

Lachish - Hebrew, an ancient Canaanite and later Israelite city and stronghold built in the 12th century BCE on the bank of Lachish River in the Judean lowlands shfela region. Lachish is now an archaeological site and moshav in modern day Israel.

Lahav - Hebrew, meaning blade. Lahav is an area in the northern Negev region comprised of a large forest, a kibbutz, and several archaeological sites.

Lakiya – Arabic, a Bedouin town founded in 1982 located in the Negev Desert north of the city of Be'er Sheva.

Leah – Hebrew, one of the four Jewish matriarchs. Leah was daughter of Lavan, sister of Rahel, first wife of Yaakov, mother of Dinah, Yehuda, Levi, Reuven, Issachar, Shimon, and Zevulun. She is buried in the Cave of the Patriarchs.

Levavot – Hebrew, hearts

Levia – Hebrew, lioness

Levite – Hebrew, a person descendant from the Jewish tribe of Levi. Levi was one of the twelve sons of Yaakov.

Levivot - Hebrew, a term taken from the book of Shmuel in the Hebrew Bible where the daughter of King David, Tamar, prepares levivot for her brother Amnon. The term is used among Sephardic and Mizrahim to describe vegetable and potato-based pancakes similar to latkes.

Livnit – Hebrew, egret. Cattle bird.

Lo hiav lihot - Hebrew, "[it/they] doesn't/don't have to be"

Ma'arat HaMachpela – Hebrew, The Cave of the Patriarchs.

Ma'arva - Hebrew, sage plant

Machpela – Hebrew, double.

Mafrum - Hebrew, a traditional Libyan dish of ground meat sandwiched between slices of potato, fried, and then cooked in a red sauce.

Malkat HaLila – Hebrew, lit. queen of the night, a species of jasmine flower that blooms only at night. The blossoms are extremely fragrant.

Mamre – Hebrew, a biblical place near Hevron at which Avram (before he was Avraham) was visited by three figures (agents of the divine).

Mamre is also the biblical place where Avraham purchased a cave and the surrounding area from Ephron the Hitti which became the Cave of the Patriarchs and was passed down to the Jews as their inheritance.

Mamshit – Hebrew/Nabataean, an archaeological site of a Nabataean caravan stop and Byzantine city along the Incense Route. Located in the Negev desert near the modern-day city of Dimona.

Matbucha - Hebrew, a traditional North African cooked condiment/salad made from tomatoes, paprika/red bell peppers, garlic, chili peppers, and olive oil. Popular in North African Jewish communities.

Mecca – Arabic, a city in the Western region of Saudia Arabia, the holiest site in Islam, birthplace of Muhammad, and site of the Kaaba, Islam's most sacred structure. A city of pilgrimage (Hajj) by millions of Muslims annually.

Medina – Arabic, a city located in the Hejaz region of Saudia Arabia, the second holiest site in Islam, the city to which Muhammad migrated from Mecca in 622 CE, and the city in which Muhammad built the first mosque known as Majid al-Nabawi (The Prophet's Mosque). Medina is the burial city of Muhammad.

Meitar – Hebrew, lit. chord such as is used to hold up a cloth tent. A yishuv located in the northern Negev desert.

Mene, Mene, Tekel, Upsharsin – The mysterious sentence written on the wall of the chamber of Belshazzar's feast. It was unable to be interpreted until captive Judean Daniel was brought from captivity and explained that "Mene" means that Gd has numbered Belshazzar's kingdom and ended it, "Tekel" means Belshazzar was weighed in the balanced (judged) and found wanting, and "Upharsin" means that Belshazzar's kingdom would be divided among the Persians and the Medes.

Met – Hebrew, dead

Mevurehet – Hebrew, a blessed woman

Miriam – Hebrew, daughter of Amram and Yocheved, sister of Moses and Aaron. Known for her leadership and fundamental role in the Jewish exodus from Egypt as well as her bravery as a nevia (prophetess).

Miriam (Mary) – Hebrew, wife of Yosef the carpenter from Natzeret (Nazareth) in Judea, mother of Yeshu (Jesus). According to Christian legend, Miriam/Mary gave birth to her son Yeshu/Jesus by immaculate conception through the Christian god and was instructed that her son would be the Jewish messiah. Miriam/Mary became a significant historical figure and Christian and Catholic religious icon.

Mizballa - Hebrew, landfill

Mizrahim – Hebrew, plural of Mizrahi, lit. "Eastern." A term used to distinguish Jews whose ancestry post-exile traces back to the Middle East and North Africa (as opposed to Jews who were exiled and fled towards Europe and the Iberian Peninsula). Mizrahi Jews have a variety of different cultural backgrounds and influences and have been subject

to persecution by non-Jews and even within Jewish communities throughout history. Most Jewish people in Israel are of Mizrachi descent.
Moshe (Moses) – Hebrew, son of Amram and Yocheved, brother to Miriam and Aaron. Husband to Tzipporah. In Judaism, when Pharoh decreed to kill all the Jewish boys born within a certain year within his kingdom to prevent the birth of the Jewish messiah, Moshe was saved by his mother and sister when they placed him in a basket in the Nile River and he was saved by Pharoh's daughter and raised as a prince within Pharoh's kingdom. As an adult, Moshe learned of his true Jewish identity and was appointed by Gd to lead the Jewish people out of slavery and exile back to the Jewish promised land of Israel. Moshe (Moses) was later appropriated as prophet and significant religious figure in both Christianity and Islam.
Moshe Dayan – Hebrew, born in 1915 in Kibbutz Degania Alef, Dayan was an influential Israeli military leader and politician who played a significant role in the founding and defense of the State of Israel. Known for his prominence in the Zionist movement and key role in several strategic wars in Israel, Dayan was also known for his controversial advocacy of compromising biblical Jewish territory in negotiations with Israel's Arab neighbors, a method used by several of Israel's leaders which has never brought about the desired and hoped for outcome of more peace in the Middle East or a stable Arab state built on that land by Arabs for Arabs.
Moznaim – Hebrew, lit. scales for weighing, the Hebrew zodiac signs that correlates to Libra. The mazal (luck sign) of the Hebrew month of Tishrei.
Muhammad – Arabic, born in Mecca in 570 CE, Muhammad is believed to be the last prophet of Allah, conveying the final "revelation" known as the Quran which he received at the age of forty in Hira cave. His teachings were compiled in the Quran and over the next 23 years of his life he preached his teachings until he gained enough followers to have his own army who would forcefully conquer and convert the Arabian Peninsula and most of the Middle East. Muhammad could be called the founder of Arab conquest and global Islamic colonization.
Mujdei – Hebrew from Romanian, a traditional Romanian condiment made from garlic, salt, and oil, though in the Middle East it is made with chopped fresh herbs like parsley and cilantro.
Nahal – Hebrew, a river
Nahal Bsor (Besor) – Hebrew, a seasonal river located in the Southern part of Israel that runs from the Judean lowlands to the Mediterranean Sea. It now serves as a partial boundary between Israel and the Gaza Strip. Nahal Bsor is mentioned several times in Judaic texts and played a significant role in Jewish history.
Nana - Hebrew, mint
Negev - Hebrew, the Negev is a desert region in the southern part of Israel, it comprises 60% of Israel's land area. It borders the Sinai

Peninsula, the Judean Hills, the Arava Valley, and Jordan and the Dead Sea. Be'er Sheva is the largest city in the Negev and dates back more than four thousand years.

Negevim – Hebrew, an invented word for people who live in the Negev.
Nesherim – Hebrew, vultures
Nevi'im – Hebrew, prophets
Nissan – Hebrew from Old Persian, a month in the Hebrew calendar that corresponds to March and April in the Gregorian calendar. Pesach is the holiday of the month of Nissan.
Nof – Hebrew, view
Oger – Hebrew, hamster
Omer - Hebrew, a yishuv in the south of Israel. Also refers to the period of 49 days that is counted between the holy days of Pesach (Passover) and Shavuot (The Feast of Weeks). Counting the Omer is one of many examples of the land-specific agricultural roots of Judaism as an ethno-religion.
Orvani - Hebrew, Eurasian jay bird, a common resident in Israel.
Otef – Hebrew, to wrap
Palestine – Greek, the origin of the word Palestine has been widely debated for years, but it is generally agreed that the name Palestine originally came from the Hebrew word *pleshet* which is mentioned more than 250 times in the Torah and roughly translates to "migratory" which refers to the seafaring Philistine people who came from the region of modern day Greece and settled along the coast near the present day Gaza Strip. During the Persian occupation of the land of Israel, ancient Judea, was first referred to as Palestine (Greek: *Palaistínē*) by Herodotus in 500 BCE. After the Romans crushed the Bar Kokhba revolt in 132 CE and Rome occupied Judea, the land of Israel was renamed *Palaestina* by the Romans to erase the indigenous Jewish connection to the land. Throughout Arab, Crusader, and Ottoman conquest and occupation of Israel the name Palestine was used to refer to the land of Israel, though during the Arab occupation it was more commonly referred to as "southern Syria" and never were Arabs living in that region referred to as Palestinians. Not until the British occupation of the land of Israel with the British Mandate of Palestine in 1920 was the area called Palestine as we know the word today and the term Palestinians at the time referred to the Jewish people who had maintained a constant presence in the land of Israel, the term Palestinian did not refer to the Arabs living in the region. Though the idea of Arab Palestinian Nationalism in the land of Israel began stirring in the 1920s, it was not solidified as the concept and national (not ethnic) identity we know it for today until the creation of the Palestinian Liberation Organization by Yassar Arafat in the 1960s after the establishment of the modern state of Israel.
Palestinian – Greek, a person from British Mandate Palestine. Prior to Yassar Arafat's invention of the Palestinian political movement, Palestinians was the term used to refer exclusively to Jewish people

living in the land of Israel during the British Mandate, the term was not associated with Arabs in the region.

Para/Parat – Hebrew, cow/ The Cow...

Paran – Hebrew, a biblical appellation for the eastern desert area of the Sinai Peninsula.

Parasha/Parashat – Hebrew, lit. portion, the weekly portion of the Torah read each week.

Pardes - Hebrew, orchard. PaRDeS is also the anacronym for Kabbalistic learning of the Torah and other Jewish texts. The acronym spells out Pshat (simple) the intended, explicit meaning of the text, Remez (hint) the alluded meaning often the symbolic or gematria equivalent of the text, Drash (seek) the homiletical or interpretive meaning, and Sod (secret) is the mystical or esoteric meaning of the text.

Pashosh – Hebrew, Graceful Prinia a warbler bird from Africa and the Levant. A term of endearment meaning "cute" or "adorable."

Passiflora -Hebrew, passionflower/passionfruit

Pesach (Passover) – Hebrew, to pass over. The Jewish holiday of Pesach is an eight-day holiday celebrated in the month of Jewish month of Nissan. Pesach commemorates the emancipation of the Jewish people from slavery and exile in biblical Egypt.

Petit pays, je t'aime beaucoup. Petit petit, je l'aime beaucoup – French, song lyrics of Petit Pays (Little Country) famously sung by Cesaria Evora as a tribute to her home country Cabo Verde, an island, peninsula country in West Africa. The lyrics translate to "Little country, I love you so much. Little, little, I like you a lot."

Petra (archaeological site) – Greek, rock. The site of Petra, originally known in Arabic as Raqmu, was the capital of the Nabatean kingdom built in the third century located in modern-day Jordan.

Pirkei de'Rabbi Eliezer – Hebrew, Chapters of Rabbi Eliezer. The Midrashic writings of Rabbi Eliezer that retell and expand upon the Torah narrative.

Pita - Hebrew, traditional Levantine flat bread

Pogrom – Yiddish/Russian, lit. devastation. The term entered the English language specifically to describe the violent attacks on Jewish people in the 19th and 20th century within the Russian Empire.

Prahim – Hebrew, flowers

Qisas al-Anbiya – Arabic, The Stories of the Prophets, a genre of literature in Islamic tradition that narrates the stories of various prophets mentioned in the Quran and other Islamic religious texts.

Qur'an – Arabic, the central religious text of Islam, believed by Muslims to be revelations from Allah conveyed to Muhammad through the angel Jabreel.

Rabeinu – Hebrew, lit. our master/teacher. A term used out of respect for learned rabbis, Torah teachers, and Jewish sages.

Rahel (Rachel) – Hebrew, the Jewish matriarch who was second daughter of Lavan, sister of Leah, second wife of Yaakov, mother of

Yosef and Benjamin. Rahel died giving birth to Benjamin and was buried near Beit Lechem (Bethlehem) in Samaria (the "West Bank").
Rakefet – Hebrew, species of cyclamen flower native to Israel.
Resolution 181 – the 1947 UN resolution dividing the land of Israel into the modern state of Israel and a modern state of Palestine for the Arabs in the locality. It was accepted by the Jews and declined by the Arabs resulting in the international recognition of the modern state of Israel and the denial of a state of Palestinian by the Arabs. The Arabs did not accept Resolution 181 because they did not want the Jews to have their own state alongside an Arab state.
Rimon - Hebrew, pomegranate
Rivka (Rebecca) – Hebrew, Jewish biblical matriarch, wife of Yitzhak, mother of Yaakov and Esav (Esau). Rivka is buried in the Cave of Machpela next to Yitzhak.
Rosh Chodesh – Hebrew, lit. "head of the month." On the full moon night of each month in the Jewish calendar, the new Jewish month begins. In biblical times, Rosh Chodesh was commemorated with animal sacrifices and shofar blasts, today Rosh Chodesh is commemorated with special blessings and small gatherings.
Rosh HaShana – Hebrew, lit. "head of the year." Rosh HaShana celebrates the birth of the universe, the day Adam and Eve were created, and is the Jewish new year celebrated on the first of Tishrei. Rosh HaShana is celebrated with special blessings, a festive meal, and food of historical and biblical significance.
Rugelach - Yiddish, lit. little twists. A traditional Jewish pastry originating in Eastern Europe traditionally sweet dairy dough shaped into crescent and filled with various sweet fillings.
Saba - Hebrew, grandfather
Sabich - Hebrew, a Levantine pita sandwich filled with fried eggplant, boiled potatoes, hard boiled eggs, pickles, tahini, chopped fresh salad, amba, and tahini.
Sabra - Hebrew, a term for a Jewish person born in Israel (as opposed to a Jewish person born in the diaspora). A sabra is also the name of a cactus commonly found in Israel, but native to Mexico.
Sakin – Hebrew, knife
Salaam elekum! Ahlan w'sahlan - Arabic, lit. "Peace upon you, hello and welcome"
Salat/im – Hebrew, salad/salads. Refers to the variety of small dishes/dips/condiments served at the beginning of a meal in Israel and throughout the Levant.
Sara (Sarah) – Hebrew, the first Jewish matriarch, the wife of Avraham, mother of Yitzhak. Sarah is buried in the Cave of Machpela next to Avraham.
Savta - Hebrew, grandmother

Sephardim – Hebrew, lit. Spain, refers to Jewish people descendant from Jews who were exiled to and lived in the Iberian Peninsula before the Spanish Inquisition in 1492.

Sela – Hebrew, boulder

Selah – Hebrew, though the exact meaning and purpose of selah in the Hebrew psalms is debated, it is generally agreed that it is a musical notation denoting an end or pause in which worshippers or congregants would say Amen or pause and reflect on the preceding words of the prayer or psalm.

Shabbat/Shabbas – Hebrew/Yiddish, the seventh day of the week in Hebrew. A holy day in Judaism, commemorated with three traditional meals, prayers, and refraining from all creative work. The Shabbat is a significant day of spiritual rejuvenation in Judaism and mirrors the seventh day of creation in which Gd rested from creative work.

Shalom – Hebrew, lit. the word peace, used in Modern Hebrew as "Hello" and "Goodbye."

Shalom, giveret, ma shlomeh? – Hebrew, "Hello, madame, how are you/how is your peace?"

Shalom, shalom baruhim habaim – "Hello, hello, welcome (lit. blessed are the arrivers)!"

Shamayim - Hebrew, sky

Sharia – Arabic, "path or "way," in Islam Sharia refers to the religious legal system derived from the Quran and the teachings of Islamic prophets.

Sharm el-Sheikh – Arabic, a town located at the southern tip of the Sinai Peninsula between the Red Sea and Mount Sinai Mountain range.

Shaul (Paul) – Hebrew (Greek), a Jew born in present day Türkiye. Known for his influence in spreading the teachings of Yeshu (Jesus) to the gentile and for his influence on the development of Christianity.

Shavuot – Hebrew, lit. weeks. The Jewish holiday which celebrates the giving of the Torah to the Jewish people at Mount Sinai. Traditionally a dairy meal is served to commemorate the time between the receiving the first written laws and the oral law that gave in depth instruction on how to observe Judaism, including the laws for the slaughtering of animals in a kosher way.

Shawati – Arabic, bank/shore of a river or stream.

Shemin zayit - Hebrew, olive oil

Shen shel shum – Hebrew, lit. "a tooth of garlic" refers to a clove of garlic.

Sheol – Hebrew, Sheol is alluded to multiple times in the Tanakh (Hebrew bible) as the "underworld" or a subterranean place to which the soul passes once a person has died. Judaism does not have a concept of "hell" or purgatory, so Sheol is assumed to be a borrowed word and concept from the ancient Assyrian culture.

Shfela/Shfelim - Hebrew, singular/plural, lit. lowlands. The shfela is a geographic region of rolling hills in south-central Israel between the Judean mountains and the coastal plains.

Shimon – Hebrew, Shimon was the second son of Yaakov (Jacob) and Leah, one of the twelve tribes of Israel.

Shir of Shirim – Song of Songs, Song of Solomon, a book of poetry in the Tanakh (Hebrew bible) written by King Shlomo (Solomon).

Shir/Shirim – Hebrew, song/songs

Shirat hadekel – Hebrew, lit. "the song of the palm tree" is a phrase coined by King Shlomo to describe the sound of the wind rushing through the fronds of the palm tree.

Shlomo HaMelech/Melech Shlomo/King Shlomo – King Solomon, third king of Israel successor to King David and BatSheva. Known for contribution of three books of poetry and writings that are a part of the Tanakh (Jewish bible). King Shlomo built the first Beit HaMikdash (holy temple). He was renowned for his wisdom and his wealth.

Shofar – Hebrew, a ram's horn trumpet used by Jewish people in their traditional ethno-religious practices and as a battle signal. Traditionally the shofar is sounded at the Jewish holy days of Rosh HaShanah and Yom Kippur.

Shofet shohet – Hebrew, lit. butchering judge.

Shomron – Hebrew, is the region of historical and biblical Samaria (Hellenized form) that shares regional borders with Judea to the south and the Galil (Galilee) to the north. Shomron was the capital of the northernmost kingdom of Israel until its capture and occupation by Assyrians, Babylonians, Persian, and other Hellenistic empires throughout history. Both Yehuda and Shomron regions are the indigenous homeland of the Jewish people but are now parts of the "West Bank."

Shtetl – Yiddish, a Jewish village primarily located in Eastern Europe and Russia.

Shuk - Hebrew, traditional open-air market

Shur – Hebrew, a biblical region located near (just east of) ancient Egypt.

Shawarma - Hebrew, a traditional Levantine meat dish consisting of layers of thinly sliced meat, stacked in the shape of an inverted cone, and slow roasted on vertical rotating spit. Traditionally served in a pita with condiments and salad.

Siddur - Hebrew, a Hebrew prayer book. Modern Hebrew for errand.

Silan – Hebrew, syrup made from date fruit.

Sinai – Hebrew, refers to the modern-day Sinai Peninsula located between Egypt and Israel. Sinai is also the name of the mountain upon which Moshe (Moses) received the Torah (Hebrew Bible).

Sivan – Hebrew from Old Persian, is the third and the ninth month in the Hebrew calendar (dependent on whether counting from the first month of the Jewish year as Tishrei or Nissan). The Jewish holy day of Shavuot is celebrated in the month of Sivan because the Jewish people received the Torah at Mount Sinai in the month of Sivan.

Suleiman – Arabic, Solomon. Common Arab male name.

Susya – Hebrew, the name of an ancient archaeological site in the Judean hills of the "West Bank" and yishuv of the same name built near the site. Ancient Susya was established in the fifth century BCE by a group of Jewish high priests (Cohenim) in the second temple period. The modern yishuv Susya near the archaeological site was established in 1982

Tamar/im – Hebrew, fruit from the date tree, date/s

Tapuz - Hebrew, orange

Tel Aviv – Hebrew, lit. Hill of Spring. Tel Aviv was established in 1909 in the Gush Dan region of Israel along the Mediterranean Sea by 60 Jewish families living in then British Mandate Palestine. Tel Aviv is now the second largest city in the modern state of Israel and a thriving hub of business and tourism.

Tel Sheva / Tel as Sabi - Hebrew/Arabic, a Bedouin town founded in 1967 situated northeast of Be'er Sheva, next to the biblical ruins of Tel Be'er Sheva.

Terumah – Hebrew, offering or tithe. The term for sacrifices and offerings the Jewish people is instructed to give to the poor or to HaShem in the Holy Temple. Terumah often refers to a portion or tithe separated from produce and crops and given to the poor.

Tevel - Hebrew, one of the seven earths mentioned in The Legend of the Jews and the book of the Zohar. Tevel is the fifth highest Earth, the one we inhabit. The Zohar first teaches that these seven earths are arranged like an onion in subsequent layers downwards into the Earth, but a second source in the Zohar teaches that these seven earths are actually the seven continents on our Earth each with its own climate and geography as well as different looking people, language, and cultures.

Thobe – Arabic, traditional Arab dress originating in the Arabian Peninsula, often worn by Arab men throughout the Middle East.

Tihon (Yam) – Hebrew, Mediterranean Sea

Timna – Hebrew, The Timna valley and archaeological site are in the Arava region of the Negev desert, north of Eilat and the Red Sea. The site and valley are composed of 15,000 acres of red desert valleys, cliffs, and the remains of the world's first copper mine, mined since the fifth century BCE.

Tinshemet – Hebrew, white screech owl, common Israel resident.

Titami – Hebrew, "taste this" directed at a female

Tlitot – Hebrew, plural. Traditional prayer shawl worn by Jewish men during prayer times.

Tohu v'Bohu – Hebrew, chaos. The state of the world before Creation as mentioned in Bereshit (Genesis 1:2). Tohu v' bohu is also used to describe a region between the lowest of the seven earths, Erez, and the sixth earth, Adama. Erez and Adama are separated by the abyss, the tohu v'bohu, a sea, and the waters, respectively.

Torah (Chumash) – Hebrew, the five books of Moshe, the five books of the Hebrew Bible, which include: Bereshit (Genesis), Shemot (Exodus), Vayikra (Leviticus), BaMidbar (Numbers),
Torat Hesed - Hebrew, lit. "Torah kindness." Found in the book of Mishlei (Proverbs) 31:26, Torat hesed is used to describe the type of wisdom the woman of valor speaks.
Tzadikim – Hebrew, plural, holy ones
Tzavoa – Hebrew, hyena
Tzedaka - Hebrew, lit. "righteousness," commonly used to refer to monetary charity, but charity in Hebrew means performing deeds of justice that bring good into the world which also includes the act of giving financial support to those in need.
Tzin – Hebrew, name for the desert wilderness in which biblical Kadesh Barnea is located. It is also the name of a mountain in the Negev that is thought to be the burial place of Aharon HaCohen (high priest Aaron). The Wilderness of Tzin (Zin) was the region extensively explored and excavated by T. E. Lawrence and C. Leanard Woolley.
Tzufit - Hebrew, sunbird, a species of nectar-eating bird from the hummingbird family, found throughout Asia and Africa.
Varod – Hebrew, pink.
Wadi – Arabic, river or watercourse. Commonly used word in modern Hebrew to refer to riverbeds that are dry for most of the year and fill with rainwater during the rainy season.
West Bank – the erroneous term for the region of Judea and Samaria (Yehuda v'Shomron).
Ya'akov – Hebrew, Patriarch of the Jewish people. Firstborn twin son of Yitzhak (Isaac) and Rivka (Rebecca), brother of Esav (Esau), husband to wives Leah and Rahel and consorts Bilha and Zilpa, father of Reuven, Shimon, Levi, Yehuda, Dan, Naphtali, Gad, Asher, Issachar, Zevulun, Yosef, Benyamin, and daughter Dinah. Yaakov adopted the sons of Yosef, Menashe and Ephraim. There is also mention of daughters in plural, but no names or details are given in the Tanakh (Hebrew Bible).
Ya'ar -Hebrew, forest
Yabbasha – Hebrew, lit. dry land. One of the seven earths mentioned in The Legend of the Jews and the book of the Zohar. Yabbasha is the mainland that contains all the rivers and springs.
Yael – Hebrew, lit. ibex, refers to the Jewish heroine mentioned in the Tanakh in the book of Judges. Yael was the righteous wife of Hever the Kenite. When the enemy general, Sisera, was fleeing the Israelite army, Yael invited him into her tent, let him fall into a deep sleep, and then killed him by hammering a tent-peg through his temple. Her actions won the war for the Jewish people. She is praised in the prophet Devorah's victory song.
Yafo – Hebrew, from the word Yafa meaning "beauty," often spelled Jaffa in English. Yafo is an ancient Canaanite port city, now a thriving

modern city located just south of Tel Aviv with a mixed population of more than 37% Arabs.

Yahadut – Hebrew, Judaism

Yam Suf – Hebrew, lit. Sea of Reeds, the Red Sea located between the Arabian Peninsula and Egypt with its northernmost shore in modern-day Israel.

Yarden (river) – Hebrew, Jordan River

Yehuda – Hebrew, the fourth son of Yaakov and Leah, the name for one of the twelve tribes of Israel, the name for the region of land apportioned to the descendants of Yehuda, the Kingdom of Judea located in modern day "West Bank."

Yehuda v'Shomron – Hebrew, Judea and Samaria, the Jewish biblical heartland and indigenous homeland of the Jewish people. The term "The West Bank" is erroneously applied to the region of Judea and Samaria.

Yerushalayim – Hebrew, Jerusalem

Yeshu – Hebrew, the Jewish son of Yosef (Joseph) and Miriam (Mary) born in the town of Beit Lechem in Judea under Roman occupation. Yeshu was raised as an observant Jewish man, but believed he was the son of Gd and the moshiach (messiah) of the Jewish people. His teachings are the basis of Christianity. In the post-biblical period, the Septuagint translated Yeshu to the Koine Greek "Iesous" which was later latinized to IESVS/Jesu and then anglicized to become the name Jesus in English.

Yishuv/yishuvim - Hebrew, living community/communities.

Yom – Hebrew, day. The Hebrew days of the week are named represented as ordinal numbers after the days of creation. The first day of the week in the Jewish calendar is on "Sunday" and is Yom Rishon (first day) and continues: Yom Sheni, Yom Shlishi, Yom Revi'i, Yom Hamishi, Yom Shishi, and the week ends with the Jewish holy day of rest, Shabbat.

Yom Hol - Hebrew, "weekday," a day that is not Shabbat or a holy day.

Yosef – Hebrew, lit. "he will add." Second-youngest son of Yaakov and Rahel, husband to Osnat, father of Menashe and Ephraim.

Z"l – A transliterated abbreviation of Jewish honorific "Zichronoam l'vracha" which means "Of blessed memory" or "May their memory be a blessing."

Za'atar – Arabic, meaning wild thyme. A Levantine seasoning mixture made from the hyssop plant (Ezov in Hebrew) traditionally mixed with sumac and sesame seeds.

Zhoug/Schoug – Arabic, a traditional Yemenite cuisine hot sauce condiment made from cilantro and green chiles brought to Israel with the return of Yemenite Jews from exile.

Ziklag – Hebrew, winding, a biblical town located in the Negev region of the kingdom/region of Judea/Yehuda. Onetime residence of David before he was king of Israel.

Zion (Tzion) – Hebrew, one of the biblical terms for Israel and Jerusalem.
Zionism – the right to self-determination of Jewish people in their indigenous homeland, the biblical and modern state of Israel.
Zionist – any person, Jewish or non-Jewish, who is a supporter of Zionism the belief that the Jewish people have a right to live in and establish a state in their indigenous homeland and every Jewish person is eligible for the right of return to Israel.

ABOUT THE AUTHOR

A.E. Hayoun is a writer, an Israel activist, and the author of The Camel in the Forest, a memoir about moving to Israel and making a home in one of the world's most misunderstood countries. Avigail writes about the complex and often times humorous aspects of life in Israel from the perspective of an American expat and a passionate Zionist. If you can't find her at her writing desk, she will be out wandering in the desert, collecting ancient pottery, and photographing camels. Avigail lives in the Negev Desert with her family.

You can subscribe for updates at www.aehayoun.com
Follow Avigail on Instagram @avigailhayoun
Write to the author at writinghayoun@gmail.com

Milton Keynes UK
Ingram Content Group UK Ltd.
UKHW031203251124
451529UK00004B/245